Tending the Garden of Our Hearts

Daily Lenten Meditations for Families

Elissa Bjeletich and Kristina Wenger

ANCIENT FAITH PUBLISHING
CHESTERTON, INDIANA

Tending the Garden of Our Hearts:
Daily Lenten Meditations for Families
Copyright © 2019 Elissa Bjeletich and Kristina Wenger

Published by:
    Ancient Faith Publishing
    A Division of Ancient Faith Ministries
    P.O. Box 748
    Chesterton, IN 46304

Old Testament quotations, unless otherwise identified, are from the Orthodox Study Bible, © 2008 by St. Athanasius Academy of Orthodox Theology (published by Thomas Nelson, Inc., Nashville, Tennessee) and are used by permission. New Testament quotations are from the New King James Version of the Bible, © 1982 by Thomas Nelson, Inc., and are used by permission.

ISBN: 978-1-944967-53-6

Printed in the United States of America

25 24 23 22 21 20 19   17 16 15 14 13 12 11 10 9 8 7 6 5 4 3 2

Contents

Fasting is wonderful because it tramples our sins like a dirty weed, while it cultivates and raises truth like a flower.

—St. John Chrysostom

Introduction

GREAT LENT IS A WONDERFUL gift, a special season designed to bring our hearts back into balance every year. We often say that the Church is a spiritual hospital. Indeed, Orthodoxy is therapeutic in nature: our Faith heals us, bringing us back to a wholesomeness in Christ so that we are physically, mentally, and spiritually well. Great Lent is an important part of this therapy, giving us an annual opportunity to prune back our passions and to refocus our energies on the spiritual life.

Whether we are aware of it or not, every home has a rhythm. When children are young, parents devise bedtime routines and morning routines, carefully creating a healthy rhythm for the children's lives. As the children grow, they begin to participate in activities outside the home: sports, music, clubs, and the like. Over the years, the family rhythm begins to follow the seasonal schedules set by coaches and teachers, and in today's American culture, the family's pace can grow hectic. Great Lent is the antidote to this problem: the Church invites us to weed through our schedules and to slow down, to refocus our attention and our hearts on growing closer to God.

As we raise our children in the Church, we must find ways to grow through the experience of Great Lent together: to fast together, to attend church together, to do works of service together, and to study together. It is our hope that these meditations will give the family something helpful to dig into and learn together, sparking conversation and helping to bring the fast to life in the home. And as we take this journey together, we'll be learning why we live out Great Lent as we do. May this holy therapy heal the hearts of our families!

How to Use This Book

WELCOME TO *Tending the Garden of Our Hearts*! We hope that you and your children will join us on our journey through Great Lent and Holy Week.

For each day, we'll offer a short reading followed by a few questions to help you engage your children in conversation about the Faith during this most important season of spiritual growth and renewal. Sometimes we'll be considering a Bible story, sometimes a saint's life story, and sometimes simply a little Lenten lesson or idea.

These are daily meditations, but sometimes that can get us into trouble. Family life can be hectic, and while some days a meditation fits in nicely, on other days . . . it does not. The Orthodox life is a struggle, and its rhythm is something like *fall down—get up—fall down—get up*. If you miss a daily meditation, or a week of daily meditations, don't be discouraged. This happens. Fall down, then get back up and move right to the current day's meditation. It's okay to miss a few. Show yourself Christ's love and mercy!

Every week, we'll be engaging a different Lenten theme. The appendix at the back of this book explains each week's theme and offers ideas for different craft projects, object lessons, and activities you might want to try, if you have the time and inclination. These extra activities are all designed to engage the family in the week's theme, but none of them are necessary. When you are able and inspired, try some. When you are not, happily skip them and move on.

We encourage you to start thinking about Great Lent ahead of time and to prepare a countdown to Pascha for your family. A countdown can be a wonderful way to bring Great Lent to life in your home. Children love a visual reminder, and Pascha takes a long time to arrive. Not every family enjoys crafts or gardening, so these are certainly optional, but we do see that especially with younger children, a countdown to Pascha can make a long Lenten season feel more exciting and its relationship to Pascha more real. In the Appendix at the back of this book, you'll find three countdown ideas: a Path to Pascha, a Blooming Wreath, and a Lenten Garden.

WEEK ONE: FORGIVENESS

Forgiveness Sunday

IN TODAY'S GOSPEL READING, JESUS gives us a special prayer
that we say all the time. We call it the Lord's Prayer or the Our
Father. There are a few different ways to translate it into English,
but it usually goes:

> *Our Father, who art in heaven, hallowed be Thy name. Thy Kingdom come,
> Thy will be done, on earth as it is in heaven. Give us this day our daily bread,
> and forgive us our trespasses as we forgive those who trespass against us, and
> lead us not into temptation, but deliver us from evil. For Thine is the kingdom
> and the power and the glory forever. Amen.*

Then Jesus said, "For if you forgive men their trespasses, your
heavenly Father will also forgive you. But if you do not forgive
men their trespasses, neither will your Father forgive your trespasses" (Matt. 6:9–15).

When Jesus says "trespasses," He means sins—offenses against
other people or against the laws of God. Jesus warns us that if
we do not forgive others for their sins, God will not forgive our
sins. If we hope to be forgiven, we must also be forgiving. That's
an interesting and important idea, so we'll be considering that
throughout this first week of Great Lent.

Forgiveness is such an important part of the fast that Great

Lent will officially begin tonight, during what we call Forgiveness Vespers. We begin the great fast by asking for forgiveness and by forgiving one another.

The service begins with the priest in his normal vestments and with the church decorated as usual. But halfway through Vespers, Great Lent will suddenly begin! So when you go, pay attention: the hymns that the chanters sing will sound sad and repentant, and then the cloths in the room will be switched out for purple cloths, and the priests and deacons will change into purple Lenten vestments. As you may know, purple is the color we use in church for Great Lent, so when you see things turn to purple, right in the middle of the service, you will know that this is the exact moment when Great Lent begins.

At the end of Vespers, we'll do our first act of Great Lent: we will ask forgiveness from our priest, and then from every single person in the church. It may sound kind of uncomfortable or awkward, but it's beautiful.

There are a few different ways to do it, but generally speaking, you'll walk right up to each person and then bow down, crossing yourself and touching the ground. You'll say, "Forgive me, a sinner!"

What if you don't think you've ever done anything wrong to them? Why would you need forgiveness?

Sometimes we annoy people, and we don't even know it. We may have distracted someone when they were trying to pray, or we may have made a joke that hurt their feelings, but we didn't even realize it. It shows humility to admit that we might have done wrong things without even knowing.

You'll say, "Forgive me, a sinner!" and the answer will be something like, "I forgive you. May God forgive us both!" or "God forgives and I forgive!"

However you are saying it at your parish, the idea is the same: we forgive each other, and we remind each other that God is forgiving. When we repent, turning away from bad things and embracing good things, God forgives us and gives us a second chance.

Great Lent is a like a wonderful second chance. Starting now, we will try to do better: to pray more, to show more love, to be more generous, and to control our appetites better. Starting now, let's try to be the best Orthodox Christians we can be for Great Lent.

If you can't go to Forgiveness Vespers, or maybe when you come back home afterward, it's a nice idea to have a special forgiveness circle with your family. After all, who do we hurt the most? Annoy the most? Say angry things to the most? Probably the people we see all the time: our family.

After you say prayers tonight, take a moment to bow before each person, saying, "Forgive me, a sinner!" They can answer just as you do in your parish, whether you say, "I forgive you. May God forgive us both!" or "God forgives; I forgive," or with words that work best for your family. Ask each person for forgiveness, and let them know that you forgive them too, so that the whole family can begin Great Lent with a clean slate.

This is such a good family tradition that you might want to do it every week during Great Lent.

⁓

What does Jesus say will happen if we do *not* forgive those who trespass against us?

Jesus says that if we do not forgive others, God will not forgive us.

When does Great Lent begin? How can you tell?

Great Lent begins during Forgiveness Vespers. You can tell because the cloths are all changed to purple, and the priest's vestments are changed to purple. Purple is the color of Great Lent.

Why would we say, "Forgive me, a sinner" to someone if we haven't done anything bad to them?

We might not even know someone, but we don't know if we have annoyed them or caused them a problem in some way. Just in case we have, we humbly say, "Forgive me, a sinner!"

FOR DISCUSSION: What's harder—asking a stranger to forgive you, or asking your family to forgive you?

Clean Monday: The First Monday of Great Lent

THE BEGINNING OF THE FAST is a good time to think about the beginning of the world. In the first book of the Bible, Genesis, we learn that when God first created the world, He saw that everything was good. He made people and saw that they were very good. All of creation began as good.

The Lord God planted a garden in Eden, with every beautiful tree that was good for food to grow from the ground. Also, in the middle of the garden there were two trees: the Tree of Life and the tree of the knowledge of good and evil. We call this garden Paradise.

The Lord God put Adam in the garden to tend and keep it, and told him, "You may eat food from every tree in the garden; but you may not eat the fruit from the tree of the knowledge of good and evil because if you do, you will die" (Gen. 2:16–17).

Adam and Eve lived happily in the garden God had created for them, never suffering or struggling. There was no hunger or pain, no sickness or death. In that perfect place, God was there with them; He would even walk and talk with them.

But God was not the only one who talked with them in the garden. The third chapter of Genesis tells us that one day, the serpent, who was very smart and very tricky, asked Eve, "Did God say, 'You shall not eat from every tree of the garden'?"

Eve said, "Well, we may eat the fruit from the other trees but not from the tree in the middle of the garden. If we do, God said that we will die."

Then the serpent said to Eve, "You will not die. God knows that you will be like gods if you eat that fruit. It will open your eyes and you will know good and evil."

So when the woman saw the tree looked pleasant and beautiful, she took its fruit and ate. She also gave it to her husband, and he ate.

After they ate the fruit of the forbidden tree, they suddenly knew they were naked. They had never noticed it before, but now they felt ashamed. So they sewed fig leaves together to cover themselves.

Then they heard the voice of the Lord God walking in the garden that afternoon, and Adam and Eve tried to hide.

God called out, "Adam, where are you?"

Adam answered, "I heard Your voice as You were walking in the garden, and I hid from you. I was afraid because I was naked."

God said, "Who said you were naked? Did you eat the fruit that I told you not to eat?"

Adam answered, "The woman You gave me offered me fruit from the tree, and I ate it."

So God said to Eve, "What have you done?"

She answered, "The serpent tricked me, and I ate the fruit."

God said to the serpent, "Because you did this, now you are cursed to crawl on your belly, and you will be eating dust all the days of your life. The woman's seed will bruise your head, and you will need to always look out for His heel."

To Eve He said, "Now that you have eaten this fruit, you will have pain when you bear children."

Then to Adam He said, "Because you followed your wife and ate the fruit I told you not to eat, now the ground will be cursed.

You will have to work very hard. All your life you will sweat, until you die and are buried in the ground from which you were made. Earth you are, and to earth you will return."

Human beings will not live forever anymore. Now life will be hard, as they will have to work for their food, and they will eventually grow old and die. God made them from the clay of the earth, and when they die, their bodies will return to the earth.

Then God said, "Behold, now the people have become like Us, knowing good and evil." Then, in case they might also take fruit from the Tree of Life, and eat it, and live forever, God sent them out of the garden. He closed the gate to the garden so that they could not come back in, and assigned the cherubim and the fiery sword that turns every way to guard the way to the Tree of Life.

After that day, Adam and Eve and all of the people who have come after them could not come back into Paradise; the gate was guarded and locked to them so that they would not eat from the Tree of Life now that they had become sinful.

Have you ever thought about how wonderful it would be to be in the Garden of Eden, in Paradise? Did you know that when Jesus was on the Cross, He said to the good thief beside Him, "I say to you, today you will be with Me in Paradise" (Luke 23:43). When Jesus died on the Cross, He went into Hades and broke down the very same gate that has kept us away from Paradise.

When we celebrate Pascha, we will be celebrating the fact that Christ has opened the gates forever and allowed us to walk with God in Paradise once more. So when we prepare ourselves for Pascha, we begin by reminding ourselves of the sinfulness that kept us away from Paradise, and we ask God's forgiveness and begin again with our efforts to live a good and prayerful life, growing always closer to God so that we too can enter into His wonderful Paradise.

⨖

What is it like in Paradise?

Paradise is very beautiful and peaceful. There is plenty of food, and there is no suffering or struggle, no work or fighting. God is present there, and you can spend time with Him.

How did the serpent trick Eve?

The serpent said that God was not telling the truth and that He wanted to keep them from being gods themselves.

Why did Adam and Eve eat the fruit of the tree of knowledge of good and evil?

Eve trusted her own judgment over God's instructions; that means that she made up her mind herself, without listening to what God had said. She liked the look of the tree and liked the idea of becoming like gods, so she ate it, and Adam followed her.

Adam blamed Eve for giving him the fruit, and Eve blamed the serpent for tricking her. Who was really to blame for Adam and Eve eating that fruit?

No one was forced to eat the fruit. Each of them chose to do it.

Why does God make them leave the garden, and why does He set up guards?

Because Adam and Eve were not yet ready for this knowledge (though eventually they would have been), they were now in a miserable state. If God allowed them to eat from the Tree of Life in their current sinful state, they would be stuck there forever, not able to grow and change to be more like God, as He wanted for them. Instead, God took pity on them and sent them out of the garden, setting a flaming sword to guard the Tree before they ate from it, so that they would grow and change into the wonderful people they were meant to be.

FOR DISCUSSION: How does our tradition of fasting relate to Adam and Eve's experience in the garden? In the garden, God offered one rule about food that Adam and Eve were not allowed to eat, but they could not follow it. God offers us a fasting rule—can we keep it? Adam was the caretaker of the animals, and he named each one of them, but he did not eat them. In the garden before the Fall, Adam and Eve ate what we would now call a Lenten diet, and they walked with God and talked easily with Him. When they fasted, they were close to God. When they broke the fast, eating food that God had forbidden, their easy afternoons of walking in the garden with the Lord came to an end. How does this relate to fasting during Great Lent?

The First Tuesday of Great Lent

OUR LORD JESUS CHRIST TOLD a parable about forgiveness, and it's recorded in the Gospel of Matthew. We call it the Parable of the Unforgiving Servant (Matt. 18:21–35), and it goes like this:

The Kingdom of heaven is like a certain king who found that some of his servants owed him money, and he wanted to get everyone to pay off their debts to him. So one at a time, the servants who owed him were brought to him, including one who owed him ten thousand talents, which was a very large amount of money. But the servant was not able to pay so much money, so his master commanded that he should be sold, with his wife and children and all that he had, so that payment could be made. The servant was very sad, and he fell down before the king, saying, "Master, please be patient with me, and give me time to pay you all that I owe." Then the master was moved with compassion, released him, and forgave the debt completely.

But that servant went out and found one of his fellow servants who owed him a very small amount of money, only one hundred denarii; and he laid his hands on him and took him by the throat, saying, "You must pay me what you owe!"

The poor servant fell down at his feet and begged him, saying, "Please be patient with me, and give me time to pay you all that I owe." And he was not moved by compassion and did not feel sorry for him at all. He just threw him into prison until the debt was paid.

So when the other servants saw that he had no compassion and put that poor man in jail, they were very upset. They went to the master and told him everything. Then the master said to him, "You wicked servant! I forgave you all of your debt because you begged me, and I showed mercy to you. Should you not also have been merciful to your fellow servant? You ask for mercy, but you do not show mercy!" The master was angry and delivered him to the torturers until he should pay all of his debt.

And Jesus told the people, "So My heavenly Father also will do to you if you do not forgive your brother from your heart."

~

Why did the master decide that he would sell his servant along with his wife and children and all that he had?

Because the servant owed him a large debt and could not pay it.

What made the master decide not to sell him?

The servant begged his forgiveness, and the master showed mercy.

Right after he was forgiven his huge debt, the servant went out to another servant who owed him a small amount of money. What did he do to that servant? Did he show mercy when the servant begged his forgiveness?

He laid hands on him and took him by the throat, saying, "Pay me what you owe!" Even though his master showed him great mercy, he showed no mercy to the servant who owed him.

FOR DISCUSSION: In the Lord's Prayer, we pray, "Forgive us our trespasses as we forgive those who trespass against us," and in the Bible we see that just after He gave us this very special prayer, Jesus said, "For if you forgive men their trespasses, your heavenly Father will also forgive you. But if you do not forgive men their trespasses, neither will your Father forgive your trespasses" (Matt. 6:15). Does this parable demonstrate the same idea? Why do you think that we can only be forgiven if we are forgiving? Why is it so important that we have forgiving hearts?

The First Wednesday of Great Lent

A S WE PURSUE OUR THEME of forgiveness, we look to the Old Testament to find a story that points us to Pascha. It's the story of Joseph, found in Genesis 37—45.

You see, Jacob had twelve sons, but he loved the one named Joseph the most. He made him a very beautiful coat of many colors, and when his brothers saw it, they were angry. They knew that their father loved Joseph more than he loved them.

Joseph was very prayerful, like his father, and he had great faith in God. God loved Joseph very much, and He would send him meaningful dreams. Sometimes those dreams predicted that Joseph would be more important than his brothers—so, naturally, his brothers did not like the dreams at all. One day, Joseph's brothers did a terrible thing: they threw him into a pit, and when some traders came by, they sold him for twenty pieces of gold. The traders took Joseph to Egypt.

The brothers needed a story to tell their father, so they killed a young goat and dipped Joseph's coat of many colors in its blood. Then they brought it to their father and pretended that a wild animal had taken Joseph away from them. Jacob was terribly sad to have lost his favorite son. All his sons and daughters tried to comfort him, but he could not be comforted.

The traders took Joseph to Egypt, and his life there was amazing and had many ups and downs. Joseph never forgot God and remained prayerful and good no matter what happened around him. God never forgot about Joseph, and He took care of him all the time. God gave Joseph a special gift so that he could understand dreams, and Joseph was able to tell everyone what their dreams meant.

One day Pharaoh, who was the leader of Egypt, had some very strange dreams, so he called for all the wise men of Egypt. He told them his dreams, but no one could guess what they meant. Then they called for Joseph, who could explain the dreams easily. Egypt was going to have some very good years with wonderful harvests, but then there would be a terrible drought, and the people would be very hungry because there was no food. God was telling Pharaoh to save the harvest from the good years so that Egypt would have food during the bad years. God used Joseph to warn Pharaoh so that God could save all of Egypt (and, as we shall see, many others as well) from the famine.

Pharaoh saw that the Spirit of God was in Joseph, and he put Joseph in charge of all of Egypt. During the good years, Joseph directed everyone to store up grain and other foods. Then the bad years came, and the harvests dried up, but in Egypt they still had food saved up.

The place where Joseph's family lived also had no food. They knew that they would starve to death without help, so the brothers traveled to Egypt to buy grain. When they met Joseph, they did not recognize their own brother, but he recognized them. He immediately knew the brothers who had hated him, even though he did nothing wrong, and had thrown him into a pit and sold him into slavery.

Joseph had every right to hate his brothers and to tell them that they must starve to pay for what they did to him. But Joseph knew God. Joseph loved God very much, and he knew that God loves all people, even when they do bad things. God wants all sinners to repent and come back to Him. God forgives, and we must forgive too.

Joseph's brothers were sorry that they had sold their brother and caused so much pain to their father, Jacob. After testing them and watching them, Joseph saw that they were sorry, and he forgave them. He said, "I am your brother Joseph, whom you sold to traders. Don't be angry with yourselves for selling me; God sent me here to save lives. This is the second year of a terrible famine, and there will be five more years. You didn't send me here, but God did, so that He could make me ruler throughout all the land of Egypt" (Gen. 45:4–8).

Even though they had done a bad thing, God had turned it into salvation. Joseph could see that God had been working all along, sending Joseph to Egypt and letting him understand dreams so that he could save Egypt and his own family. Joseph could be a part of God's plan because he was righteous. He was prayerful and good, so he could understand God's messages about dreams, and he was forgiving and merciful, which allowed him to save his family.

The Fathers say that Joseph is so much like Jesus because he is so good and prayerful, and he delivers all of Israel and Egypt from death—just as Jesus Christ delivers all of us from death. God allowed Joseph to be betrayed, as Jesus was betrayed, and to be "dead" in the eyes of his family, just as Jesus died and went down into Hades—so that God could show that He was not dead but was bringing salvation to the people.

꒱

Why didn't Joseph's brothers like him? What did they do to him?

The brothers did not like Joseph because he was their father's favorite son, and his dreams seemed to promise that he would be more important than them. They sold Joseph to traders and lied to their father, saying that a wild animal had eaten Joseph, because they were jealous.

How did Joseph know what people's dreams meant?

God told Joseph the meaning of dreams.

What did Pharaoh's dreams mean?

Pharaoh's dreams meant that Egypt would need to store up food during the good years so that they would have something to eat during the bad years.

Why did Pharaoh trust Joseph to be in charge of Egypt?

Pharaoh believed that Joseph was wise and saw that God was blessing him. He wanted God to bless Egypt too, so he put Joseph in charge.

Did Joseph forgive his brothers for selling him to the traders?

Yes, Joseph forgave them and said that God had caused it to happen so that Joseph could make sure that his family and so many others did not starve during the seven bad years.

FOR DISCUSSION: Together, list all the ways Joseph is like Jesus.

The First Thursday of Great Lent

A S WE CONSIDER FORGIVENESS, WE come to the holy St. Dionysius, who was born and raised on the beautiful Greek island of Zakynthos. He is very famous for a situation where he forgave someone whom most people would find very hard to forgive.

You see, Dionysius was born to wealthy Christian parents, and they raised him to love God. While he was still young, he chose to become a monk. He grew holier and holier over the years, and he was chosen to be the Archbishop of Aegina. He took care of Aegina for a long time, and then eventually he retired and moved back to a monastery on the island of Zakynthos.

Now, back on Zakynthos, you see, there were two families who were always feuding, always fighting with each other. They battled all the time, and people were always getting hurt. One was Dionysius's family, the Sigourou family, and the other was the Moninou family. In one of the battles between the two families, St. Dionysius's own brother, Konstantinos, was murdered.

The murderer ran to the saint's monastery and asked to be hidden away because the Sigourou family was searching everywhere to find him and kill him. Naturally, the monastery was always a safe place for people, so the monks took him in to protect him. Later, he asked to confess to St. Dionysius, who of course said prayers with him and heard his confession. The man confessed that he had killed Konstantinos Sigourou, the saint's own brother.

Saint Dionysius was so very sad to hear that his brother was dead. Now he understood why his family was trying to kill this man. Saint Dionysius was sorry to lose his brother, and he was saddened to see human beings murdering each other. He hid the murderer in the monastery so that he would not be killed by the saint's family, and when he was able to do so, St. Dionysius helped the man escape.

Can you imagine helping the man who murdered your brother escape from your own angry and hurt family members?

Remember that St. Dionsyius was a priest and a man of God. Whenever we do something wrong, God wants us to repent our sin and change our ways, coming back to Him and to His Church. God loves even murderers, and God has asked us to love our enemies. Holy St. Dionysius understood this.

Saint Dionysius's family wanted to kill this man, and if they did, how could the murderer ever repent of his sins as God wants? Also, if they killed this man, then they would also be murderers, and everything would just get worse. The fighting between these two families would just get more and more terrible.

As God asks all of us to do, St. Dionysius forgave the man who had killed his brother. He helped him escape safely so that his own family could not make things worse by killing him.

Many years later, the murderer returned to the monastery and was repentant for the sin he had committed. When he learned that the monk who saved him was Konstantinos's own brother, he was amazed and decided to stay with these wonderful monks, becoming a monk himself and repenting for the rest of his days for the life he had taken.

God wants every sinner to repent and to come home to Him, and surely if St. Dionysius had not been forgiving, this man would never have had time to repent or to become a monk himself. It must have been hard to forgive this man, but because of St. Dionysius's Christian heart, many lives—and souls—were saved by this one beautiful act of forgiveness.

ॐ

Why was the Sigorou family trying to kill the man who showed up at the monastery?

The two families were fighting, and this man killed Konstantinos Sigourou, and the family wanted to take revenge.

What did St. Dionysius do when the man confessed that he had murdered Konstantinos?

He forgave him, protected him, and helped him escape to safety.

What good things came from St. Dionysius's forgiveness?

Because he forgave him and helped him escape, the Sigourou family was not able to kill the man. Because of this, the fighting between the families stopped before more people were killed. Also, the murderer was able to live to repent his crime, as God desires.

When the man came back to the monastery, he was surprised. Why? What did he decide to do?

He was surprised to learn that the man who forgave him and helped him was actually Konstantinos's brother. He was so impressed with the saint's holiness that he become a monk at the same monastery.

FOR DISCUSSION: If you try throwing a pebble into a pond of water, you'll see that the pebble falls in, and then circles of waves, called ripples, spread out from that one pebble. One little pebble causes so many ripples! We can see how St.

Dionysius's act of forgiveness had a kind of ripple effect, making other good things happen. Does forgiveness always have this effect? What kind of ripple effects do we set off when we forgive?

The First Friday of Great Lent

WE HAVE SEEN AMAZING EXAMPLES of holy people who forgave tremendous crimes, like Joseph, who forgave the brothers who sold him into slavery, and holy St. Dionysius, who forgave the man who killed his own brother.

It can be very difficult to forgive much smaller transgressions than these. We know that if we hope God will forgive us our trespasses, we must forgive those who trespass against us, and yet this is not easy. Today we are going to think about an interesting strategy that can help us grow more humble and forgiving.

Let's imagine that there are two brothers, and they are fighting. The older brother complains: "I am always helping my younger brother do things, but he always gets mad and yells at me. He never appreciates my help. He's terrible to me!" We might ask the younger brother why they are always fighting and get a different answer: "Every time I try to do something by myself, my older brother jumps in and tries to do it for me. He thinks I am a baby and can't do anything myself. He's terrible to me!" These two brothers could stay mad for a very long time. What is the problem?

The Church Fathers might tell us that the problem is that these boys are each looking at their brother's sins and not at their own. Each of them is mad about his brother, but really neither one is listening to what the other says, and both are only thinking about how mad they are. It's hard to forgive when all we can see is what the other person has done wrong.

What the older brother needs to say is, "My little brother gets mad when I try to help. He says that he does not want my help but wants to try this on his own, and I keep forcing my help on him. This hurts my brother."

What the younger brother needs to say is, "My older brother gets mad when I refuse his help. He is hoping to teach me and to show me how smart and helpful he can be, but instead of thanking him for being helpful, I get angry and yell at him. This hurts my brother."

If the brothers could think about how the other one feels and listen to exactly what the other one is saying, they could see that they are both hurting each other. They should say to themselves, "Instead of thinking about what my brother is doing, I should stop and think about what I am doing."

When we only focus on what the other person does wrong and we never blame ourselves, then the angry fighting just goes on and on. But we can fix it if we stop and ask ourselves, "What am I doing wrong?" In most cases, *both* people are doing something wrong. When we see that both of us are wrong, it is much easier to be forgiving.

But what if you are fighting with your brother, and you really think about your own behavior and take his words very seriously, and you really search your heart, but you find that you really are not doing anything wrong at all? What will help us forgive then?

The very wise Abba Dorotheos teaches us that if a person really takes the time to prayerfully think about his own thoughts and actions, he will usually find that he *did* do something wrong, whether it was by doing something or saying something, or even by his attitude or the way he was acting. But if the person really searches and searches and cannot find that he did anything wrong at all, it is likely that he can think of some other time when he has done something wrong. Maybe there was a time when he hurt or annoyed this person, or maybe some other person. At some time, he probably did something he should not have. If he really tries, he will always find cause for being humble and admitting that he is not perfect.

So let's imagine another case: this time it is two sisters who are fighting. The younger sister was sitting quietly on the couch reading a little book when her older sister came in, sat right beside her, and started to read over her shoulder, which can be very annoying. The younger sister asked her politely to stop, so the older sister decided to amuse herself by pulling her little sister's hair. Each girl said the other girl was more annoying, but the truth is that if you really examine the situation, the younger sister is innocent here. All she has done is read a book and speak politely, and her older sister has been intentionally annoying her.

How can the younger sister ever forgive her older sister?

Well, perhaps the younger sister can try to remember a time when she annoyed her older sister or her friend or her mother. If she searches her heart enough, she'll find a time when she offended someone. If she can remember how easily she fell into a sin like that, and how much she hopes to be forgiven, this will help her forgive her sister.

Sometimes, when we ask someone to forgive us, we say, "Please forgive me. I was wrong to do that, but I did it because you . . ." That is not a good apology. We need to think only about what we have done wrong, not about what someone else did wrong. A good apology speaks only of our own sins. We're not responsible before God for the other person's sins; we are only responsible for our own sins.

Remember how Adam and Eve blamed others for the bad choice they made in the garden? God did not punish them for another's bad choices. He punished each of them for their own bad choices.

Too often, we wait to ask forgiveness until the other person has asked forgiveness. What if both people wait forever? We should always be quick to ask forgiveness and to forgive so that we can keep our hearts focused on God instead of tied up in anger.

With forgiveness in our hearts, we can receive forgiveness, and we can participate in God's wonderful work here on earth.

૱

Why do the Fathers tell us to think about our own sins? Why does that help us forgive?

When we think about other people's sins, it is easy to judge and hard to forgive, but when we admit that we are sinful too, it is much easier to forgive other sinners.

Why shouldn't we say "but" or talk about another person's sins in our apologies?

An apology should speak only of our own sins. After all, we're not responsible before God for the other person's sins; we're only responsible for our own.

FOR DISCUSSION: Learn the Lenten Prayer of St. Ephraim:

O Lord and Master of my life! Take from me the spirit of laziness, idle curiosity, lust for power, and vain talk. (+ Prostration)

But give rather the spirit of chastity, humility, patience, and love to Your servant. (+ Prostration)

Yea, Lord and King! Grant me to see my own faults and not to judge my brother, for You are blessed unto ages of ages. Amen. (+ Prostration)

As you can see, St. Ephraim teaches we should first repent our own sins, then ask God to help us do better, and finally ask Him to help us look at our own sins: "Grant me to see my own faults and not to judge my brother." This is a wonderful prayer for every day of Great Lent.

Consider the Prayer of St. Ephraim, and discuss situations where looking at your own sins might have been a good strategy to help you forgive.

The First Saturday of Great Lent

THERE IS ANOTHER SAINT WHO was well known for for-giveness. He was an Egyptian monk named Doulas, and he led a difficult life. He was known for being meek, humble, and obedient—and because of this, the other monks mocked him and bullied him every day.

At first it was difficult for him, but gradually, by praying to God and humbling his soul, he reached the point where he could feel sorry for his abusers with all his heart and pray for them. Have you ever prayed for someone who was mean to you? God asks us to pray for our enemies, because mean people really need our prayers to help their hearts soften so they will repent, and also because when we pray for someone we begin to see them as God sees them. We begin to love them and to feel sad for them because they are so twisted up and mean and unhappy.

One day a monk stole and hid some valuable things from the monastery's cathedral. During the investigation, some of the monks accused St. Doulas, because they didn't like him. The hum-ble monk tried to defend himself, but some of the other monks were saying that they saw him take the vessels. When St. Doulas saw that nobody would believe him, he stopped arguing and said, "Forgive me, holy fathers; I am a sinner." Everyone believed he was guilty. The abbot of the monastery ordered that they take away St. Doulas's monk's robes and dress him in regular clothes. Sobbing bitterly, St. Doulas prayed, "Lord Jesus Christ, Son of God, because of Your Holy Name I clothed myself in monastic garb, but now, through my sins, it is stripped from me."

Saint Doulas was placed in chains, and the steward demanded to know where the stolen items were hidden, but he only repeated, "Forgive me, I have sinned."

Then they turned him over to the civil authorities for trial, and they tortured him, but the saint kept repeating that he did not have the stolen items. The city leaders asked the monks what to do with him, since they had delivered him over to the courts. They answered, "Do with him as the laws prescribe." The saint was sentenced to have both his hands cut off. Before they cut his hands off, the governor asked again to hear where the stolen things were. The saint answered, "Governor, do you want me to confess something that I did not do? I do not want to tell lies about myself, since every lie is from the devil." They took the saint to the terrible place where they would cut off his hands.

Saint Doulas did not complain throughout any of his tortures or punishments, even though he was innocent of the crime. He remained humble and prayerful and quiet throughout the whole ordeal, which is why today he is called St. Doulas, the Passion-Bearer of Egypt. A passion-bearer is a person who faces death and suffering in a Christlike way, quietly and humbly, without anger or complaint.

Finally, at the last minute, the real thief felt bad about the punishments St. Doulas was receiving, and he went to the abbot to confess that he had committed the crime, so St. Doulas did not lose his hands.

After twenty years of exile and humiliation, St. Doulas was allowed to return to the same monastery where he was abused and mocked, accused of a crime he did not commit, and handed to the authorities for trial and torture. Can you imagine what it would feel like to come back to a place like that? Can you imagine how St. Doulas must have felt, looking at those monks who had been so cruel?

All of the monks began to ask St. Doulas to forgive them. What do you think he did?

Amazingly, St. Doulas was not angry with them at all. He wasn't upset at all. Instead, he was grateful. He thanked those monks for doing him a favor. What was that favor?

Saint Doulas thanked them for giving him the chance to suffer innocently as Christ did. The saint had suffered greatly, but throughout his suffering he prayed to God and grew ever closer to Him—so in the end, the sufferings had made him holier.

The saint thanked the people who had harmed him, and then he asked the Lord to forgive them.

After three days they found the saint had died while kneeling at prayer. His body was locked in the cathedral, and his burial was delayed until the arrival of the abbot and monks from a nearby monastery. When they arrived, everyone gathered for the funeral and went into the church, and they saw that the body of St. Doulas was not in the cathedral. Only his clothes and sandals remained. Everyone understood that the Lord was showing them that they were not worthy to bury this great saint, because they had believed that he was a sinner and a thief.

~

The other monks teased and mocked and abused St. Doulas. Why?

Because he was meek, humble, and obedient. All of these are actually very good qualities, but they were not meek and humble and obedient and didn't see those as good qualities at all.

Another monk stole some church vessels and hid them. Why did they think St. Doulas did it?

> *The monks hated St. Doulas, so they said he did it. Saint Doulas tried to defend himself, then stopped arguing and said, "Forgive me, holy fathers, I am a sinner." They thought he was confessing to taking the vessels.*

What was the punishment for stealing?

> *Saint Doulas was chained, tortured, and sentenced to have his hands chopped off. (At the last minute, the real thief confessed.)*

When St. Doulas returned to his old monastery, how did he react to the monks who had treated him so badly? What did he say to them?

> *Saint Doulas forgave them and said that he was grateful that they gave him an opportunity to grow closer to God through innocent suffering. He prayed that God would forgive them as well.*

What miracle occured after the saint's death?

> *Saint Doulas's body disappeared from the locked cathedral.*

FOR DISCUSSION: It is hard to imagine a person who could be treated so badly for so long, but who could then easily forgive people who bullied, attacked, and falsely accused him. There is another famous saint, St. Seraphim of Sarov, who was beaten so badly by robbers that he was permanently bent over for the rest of his life. But when the police caught them, he asked them to forgive them and not to punish them for their crimes. These holy saints truly forgave their attackers. What do you think makes that possible?

The Sunday of Orthodoxy

THE ICONOCLASTIC CONTROVERSY BEGAN IN the year
726. The iconoclasts were people against icons, and they
wanted all of the icons removed from the Church and destroyed.
They believed that making images of God was forbidden because
of the commandment that says: do not worship graven images.
The iconoclasts were concerned that people were worshiping the
icons just as the pagans worshiped statues. Pagans believe that the
statues are gods, but do the Orthodox believe that icons are gods?

Those who loved icons argued that, in the Old Testament, the
understanding was that you cannot see God, so you could not
make images of Him. But the Old Testament ends just before
the birth of Jesus Christ. Once Jesus Christ was born, something very important changed: God had a body. Jesus Christ
is God, and He has a visible human body that can be touched
and wounded and crucified. Once He took on a human body, we
could make images of it.

They also argued that people should not worship icons, but
instead that they could venerate them. Worshiping an icon would
mean that you thought the icon itself—the wood and the paint—
had some kind of magical power or was like a god. On the other
hand, venerating is showing respect to an icon that passes along

to the real person shown in the icon. So if you kiss an icon of Jesus and say a prayer, you understand that the real Jesus Christ is receiving your kiss and your prayer. You are not kissing and praying to wood and paint, but kissing and praying to the actual Jesus who is in heaven and who you are seeing in the icon. We are not worshiping icons themselves but simply venerating the holy ones we see in them.

In some cases, people were going too far with icons. The Church needed to talk about icons and make it clear what was okay and what was not okay. But the iconoclasts were not just talking; they began a persecution, killing the Christians who defended icons. More Christians were killed for defending icons than all of the Christians who died in the persecutions in the early Church, when the terrible Roman emperors would torture and kill them for being Christians. But now it was not pagans killing Christians; it was Christians killing Christians.

When an iconoclast named Leo the Isaurian became emperor, he removed the holy Patriarch Germanus from his throne at the head of the Church and sent him to prison. The emperor announced that all of the icons must be taken away and destroyed—from churches, from public spaces, and even from people's homes. Even the copper wonderworking icon of our Lord Jesus Christ that was above the Copper Gates in Constantinople was to be removed and destroyed.

The people were upset to lose this beloved icon. An outraged crowd gathered at the Copper Gates as the soldiers climbed a ladder to remove the beloved icon. Many people in the crowd rushed toward the ladder, and it toppled to the ground, killing the soldier who had been standing at the top.

The emperor executed many faithful Christians as a result of this situation, most of whose names we do not know. We do know that Julian, Marcian, John, James, Alexius, Demetrius, Leontius, Photius, and Peter were locked up in prison and kept there for about eight months, each day receiving five hundred blows. They stayed alive through this only through the power of Christ and bravely endured their sufferings.

By order of the emperor they were burned with a red-hot iron, and their heads were cut off. Saint Maria the Patrician, a wealthy woman who had been present on the day that the ladder fell, learned about their executions and voluntarily accepted a martyr's death. The bodies of the martyrs were buried in a coastal area near the church of the holy Martyr Theodore, and 139 years later, it was discovered that none of them had decayed; they were incorrupt. This is how God sometimes lets us know that someone is indeed a very holy saint.

Over those years many good Christians were killed for defending icons. People took the beautiful icons out of churches and hid them in their homes to protect them, at the risk of death to themselves and their families.

More than one hundred years after the trouble at the Copper Gates, a council of all the bishops and patriarchs decided that icons could be used in church, that they could be venerated but never worshiped, and that icons celebrate the Incarnation of our Lord Jesus Christ (which means that He truly has a human body). Icons were officially restored to the Church on the first Sunday in Lent. Many families brought wonderful icons out of hiding in their attics and walls and placed them back in the churches where they belonged. Ever since, this first Sunday of Great Lent has been commemorated as the Triumph of Orthodoxy.

We celebrate the return of the icons, the victory over iconoclasm, but we are celebrating more. The victory of the icons is actually the victory of the truth that our God became man. He took on a specific human body at a specific time in history, and this specific Jesus Christ is truly the Word of God and is the One who was crucified and the One who tramples down death by death. When we celebrate the Triumph of Orthodoxy, we celebrate the spreading of the truth, that God became a man who was nailed to a Cross and who rose from the dead, and that man chose twelve apostles and gave them the power to preach His gospel to the whole world. Christ Himself built our Church and presides over it today. That is the Triumph of Orthodoxy!

This is a triumph that makes us so happy we might shout. On this first Sunday of Great Lent, Orthodox people all over the world carry icons in processions and loudly declare:

This is the Faith of the Apostles, this is the Faith of the Fathers, this is the Faith of the Orthodox, this is the Faith which has established the universe.

Today only, no one will mind if you shout that out in Church. Today is a day to celebrate Christ's victory and His Church's triumph.

࿉

Why did the iconoclasts think you could not make an image of God, and why do the Orthodox say that you can make them?

In the Old Testament, they could not make images of God because God cannot be seen. The Orthodox argue that after the Old Testament, when the Son of God took on a human body, then people could see Him and make images of Him.

Iconoclasts argued that people were worshiping icons. Would that be good?

No, that would not be good. It is good to venerate an icon, which means that you can kiss and pray to an icon while understanding that the person or angel in the icon in heaven is really the one you are kissing and praying to. It is not good to worship an icon, which means thinking that the icon itself is powerful. Even a wonder-working icon is not doing miracles by itself, but through the prayers of the person in the icon and through the power of Jesus Christ.

What happened when the soldiers came to take away the icon above the Copper Gates in Constantinople?

A crowd gathered, and they were very upset. When the crowd moved toward the ladder a soldier was standing on, the ladder fell, and the soldier died. Many Christians were martyred for this, and some were tortured for eight months and then martyred.

FOR DISCUSSION: When we talk about how the Orthodox Faith has not changed much over the years, what we are really saying is that many Christians fought and died to keep the teachings of the Church the same, to preserve the Faith of our Fathers and the Faith that the holy apostles handed down to us. Can you imagine having to fight to keep the Church from changing to a false teaching? Because of those holy people who fought for the icons and who put their lives on the line for the Church, we can carry icons in processions and pray in churches with beautiful icons on all of the walls. We should say a prayer of thanksgiving to those holy saints who preserved the Faith for us, and we should pray for strength to make sure that we pass down the true Faith to those who come after us.

The Second Monday of Great Lent

THIS WEEK WE WILL BE exploring the theme of Orthodoxy; we'll think about many of the things that make our worship so special. Yesterday was the Sunday of Orthodoxy, and we celebrated the return of icons to our Church, so it seems appropriate to discuss icons today.

In the fourth century, Bishop Eusebius wrote down the entire history of the Church as it was known at the time. He tells us all about the first three hundred years of Church history. Eusebius tells us that the first-ever icon was made while Jesus Christ was still alive.

At that time, a man named Abgar ruled in Edessa. His whole body was covered with leprosy. That's a terrible disease that rots the body and makes body parts actually fall off—and to make it worse, it's contagious, and back then they had no cure. So people with leprosy were usually sent away together and made to stay away from everyone else while they suffered and died.

Now, Jesus was healing many people, including people with leprosy, and reports of the great miracles Jesus was working were spreading, and they reached poor Abgar. Even though he had never seen Jesus, he believed that this was the Son of God, and that Jesus could heal him. He wrote a letter to Jesus, asking him to come to Edessa to heal him, and he sent his own portrait-painter, Ananias, to take the letter to Jesus and to paint His portrait.

Ananias arrived in Jerusalem and saw the Lord surrounded by people. There were so many people pressing around Him that Ananias could not get anywhere near Him. Ananias stood on a high rock and tried to paint the portrait of the Lord Jesus Christ from afar, but it wasn't going well. Jesus saw him up on that rock and called out, "Ananias!" He knew his name! Jesus talked with Ananias and explained that He could not spend days sitting to be painted, but He did give Ananias a short letter for Abgar in which He praised this ruler's strong faith. He also promised to send His disciple to heal him of his leprosy and to guide him to salvation.

Jesus knew that Ananias was supposed to paint His portrait, but He could not possibly sit still for several days to be painted—His ministry was too important to stop.

Then the Lord asked that water and a cloth be brought to Him. He washed His Face, and then He dried it with the cloth, and His Holy Face was imprinted on the cloth. Ananias took the cloth and Jesus' letter back to Edessa. Reverently, Abgar pressed the holy object to his face, and his leprosy was mostly healed. Just a small bit of leprosy stayed with him until the disciple Jesus had promised came to him. Jesus sent him St. Thaddeus, one of the seventy apostles who preached the gospel throughout the world. He came and completed the healing of Abgar and then baptized him and the people of Edessa.

Abgar took the cloth with Jesus' image on it, which is called the Holy Napkin, and he placed it in a gold frame adorned with pearls and placed it in a niche over the city gates. On the gateway above the icon he inscribed the words, "O Christ God, let no one who hopes on You be put to shame."

For many years, the people of Edessa always bowed down in front of the Icon Not-Made-by-Hands whenever they passed through the gate. But many years later, one of the great-grandsons of Abgar was worshiping idols, so he took the icon off the city wall. God sent the Bishop of Edessa a vision and said to hide His icon. The bishop came at night, lit a lampada before it, and walled it up with a board and with bricks.

Many years passed, and the people forgot about the Icon Not-Made-by-Hands. But in the year 545, an enemy army attacked the city, and it looked as if they would surely be defeated. The Most Holy Theotokos appeared to the bishop and ordered him to remove the icon from the little sealed space where it was kept in the wall, because it would save the city from the enemy. The bishop opened the wall and found the Icon Not-Made-by-Hands. In front of it, the lampada was still burning, and on the board that had closed it in, a copy of the icon was reproduced. The joyful bishop and his clergy processed with the Icon Not-Made-by-Hands all around the city, and the invading army simply withdrew and went home.

During the time of the iconoclast heresy, when the faithful were dying to defend icons in the Church, those who loved icons sang the Troparion to the Icon Not-Made-by-Hands. In a letter arguing that icons should be venerated, Pope Gregory II pointed out to the Byzantine emperor that the healing of King Abgar and the history of the Icon Not-Made-by-Hands at Edessa is a commonly known fact. Jesus Himself created the first icon; He miraculously transferred the image of His face onto the Holy Napkin, which then healed Abgar's leprosy and protected the city he loved.

ॐ

Why did Abgar want to send for Jesus?

He had heard stories about Jesus and the miracles He worked and believed that He was the Son of God and could heal his leprosy.

Why did Abgar send a portrait artist to Jesus?

He wanted a portrait of the Son of God.

How does this story show that Jesus approved of the idea of icons?

If Jesus did not approve of icons, He would have told Ananias that it is forbidden to make a portrait of the Lord. Instead, He made the first icon Himself by wiping his face with the Holy Napkin.

FOR DISCUSSION: One of the main reasons we defend the veneration of icons is because of the Incarnation. The Son of God took on human flesh and lived among us. He took on an actual human body—and a very specific body at a specific time in history. Making the image of Christ recognizes and affirms this important reality. The icon emphasizes the Incarnation of Jesus Christ, and therefore it points us to the basic Christian truth that the One whose death and Resurrection we celebrate on Pascha is in fact the Word of God who became human in Jesus Christ. Can you see how icons and the Incarnation are related?

The Second Tuesday of Great Lent

W E ARE EXPLORING THE THEME of Orthodoxy; we'll
consider many of the things that make our worship so
special. Today we're thinking about how we Orthodox worship
with all of our senses and our whole bodies. Why do we do that,
and how?

As we prepare ourselves for Pascha, let's think about Christ's
Resurrection. As we know, our Lord was crucified and died on
a Cross, and on the third day when the women went to the tomb,
they found that it was empty. The linen cloths and the handker-
chief that had been around Christ's head were folded and left
behind in the tomb, but His body was not, because Christ resurrected bodily. Forty days later, when He ascended up to heaven,
He took that body with Him—not only did God take on human
flesh on earth, but He carried that human flesh right up to
heaven.

Christ's Resurrection is not the end of the story. The joy of
the Resurrection is not just that Christ resurrected, but that we
will too. There will be another resurrection in the future, at the
time we call the Second Coming—this is what we mean when we
say in the Creed, "and He will come again in glory to judge the
living and the dead. His Kingdom shall have no end." Someday,
Christ will come back, and all human beings from all of history
will be resurrected too. Abraham and Noah and you and me, and

everyone who ever lived, will be resurrected when Jesus Christ comes back to us, and we will all have our bodies. Our bodies will be different, because they will not feel hot or cold; they won't get sick, and they won't die. They will be different from our bodies now, but they'll still be our bodies.

Some people think that you are really just a soul and that you are somehow trapped in a body, but truly you are both your body and your soul together. When we die, we will be separated from our bodies for a time, but when Christ returns, we will have our bodies again.

Our bodies have a big effect on us. When we are sick, it can be hard to think. When we are very tired, it can be hard to pray— we might fall asleep even though we are trying to pray. It can be hard to pray when we are lying down, but it is easy to stay awake and to keep praying if we stand up. What about when we are very full of food? Have you ever noticed that after a big Thanksgiving dinner, people seem to want to lie around on couches and relax? We get kind of sleepy and lazy when we eat a lot of rich foods. It should not surprise us that when we want to be more prayerful during Lent, we don't eat all of those rich foods. Our bodies play an important part in our spiritual lives.

God made us, so He understands how we work, and He designed our worship in a way that really works for the way we are built. Our Orthodox worship always involves our whole bodies and all of our senses, because our bodies are a part of us.

So why do we Orthodox worship with our bodies? Because we know the joy of the Resurrection, and we know that our bodies and our souls are forever connected, so we must use both of them to worship God and to develop healthy spiritual lives.

How do we use both body and soul in worship?

We use our five senses:

» We see the icons and the light of the candles.
» We smell the incense.
» We hear the beautiful chanting and the ringing of the bells.
» We touch our fingers together and make the sign of the cross.
» We taste the Body and Blood of Christ.

We stand up, and we kneel down. We cross ourselves and touch our hearts or touch the floor. We prostrate ourselves on the floor. We trace a cross in holy oil on each other's foreheads. We watch the acolytes process, and we run our fingers over carved wood and embroidered linens. Our eyes feast on the rich colors of the icons.

Through all of this, we are helping to focus ourselves on the prayers we are offering up to God, and we keep our bodies and our souls united in the joy of moving ever closer to Christ.

ॐ

Are human beings really just souls that are trapped inside bodies?

No. Human beings are both soul and body, together.

When we die, our bodies will be buried, and our souls will leave them behind. When will our souls be reunited with our bodies?

When Christ comes back at the Second Coming, all human beings who ever lived will be resurrected with their bodies.

Can you name three ways that your body participates in Orthodox worship?

(There are many answers, but they might include: smells incense, crosses self, stands, kneels, prostrates, hears chanting, sees icons, etc.)

FOR DISCUSSION: We don't know when Christ will return, and we don't know much about what our bodies will be like. Do you ever wonder what it will be like at the Second Coming? From the last chapters of the Gospel of John, we do have a little bit of information on Christ's resurrected body—for example, He ate fish after He resurrected. It seems that He could pass through closed doors. The Apostle Thomas was able to stick his hands into Christ's wounds—so Christ still had wounds, and He could be touched in His resurrected body. We don't know for sure that our resurrected bodies will be like Christ's was. What do you think? To know for sure, we will have to wait and see.

The Second Wednesday of Great Lent

W E ARE EXPLORING THE THEME of Orthodoxy, thinking about many of the things that make our worship so special. Today we're thinking about the sign of the cross.

When our Lord Jesus Christ conquered death by death, the method of His death was the Cross. Crucifying people was a punishment used in those days, designed to humiliate, torture, and kill criminals. But when Christ is put to death on the Cross, He conquers death. For Christians, the cross changes from an instrument of death to the life-giving Holy Cross. For this reason, we decorate our churches with crosses, we wear crosses on our bodies, and we make the sign of the cross with our hands.

Christians have been making the sign of the cross since the beginning. In the second century, Tertullian wrote, "In all our travels and movements, in all our coming in and going out, in putting on our shoes, at the bath, at the table, in lighting our candles, in lying down, in sitting down, whatever employment occupieth us, we mark our foreheads with the sign of the cross." He even said, "We Christians wear out our foreheads with the sign of the cross." Back then, Christians would cross themselves with just one finger on their foreheads.

Today, we make the sign of the cross by bringing the tips of the first three fingers together (the thumb, index, and middle ones) to represent the Holy Trinity (Father, Son, and Holy Spirit), and bending the last two (the ring and little fingers) against our palms to signify the dual natures of Christ: He is fully God and fully man.

The Holy Great Martyr Barbara lived at the beginning of the fourth century, and in her life story we hear of a miracle involving the sign of the cross. Her father, the pagan Dioscorus, was a rich man. His wife had died, leaving him just his one beautiful daughter, Barbara. Concerned that she was perhaps too beautiful, Dioscorus put her in a tower to keep her protected and hidden away. Only her teachers were allowed to see her.

From the tower windows, Barbara had a beautiful view. She looked out on the hills and their swiftly flowing rivers and flowery meadows. At night, she saw the stars twinkling. She concluded that the God who created such a beautiful world must be real and immense—not some statue made by human beings like her father worshiped, but truly a real God of infinite power.

As word of her great beauty spread throughout the city, many young men asked to marry her. But she refused to marry anyone. Dioscorus thought that maybe she had become strange from spending so much time alone in the tower, so he let her come out and live in the city. There, she met some young Christian women, and they taught her all about the Holy Trinity. Christians were being persecuted, so everything was kept very secret—but it happened that a priest from Alexandria traveled through town, and he taught her about the Faith and baptized her before heading back to his homeland.

Dioscorus was building a bathhouse with two windows on the south side. But he went out of town on business, and while he was away, Barbara approached the workers and asked them to make a third window so that it would have three, to glorify the Holy Trinity.

Barbara stood beside the bathhouse, and on one of the walls she traced the sign of the cross with her finger. Amazingly, the cross was deeply etched into the marble, as if she had carved it with iron. Later, her footprints were imprinted on the stone steps of the bathhouse. There were more miracles, as the water of the bathhouse healed many people.

When Dioscorus returned to town and found that his bathhouse had the wrong number of windows, Barbara told him that she had come to know the Holy Trinity. She spoke to him of Jesus Christ and told him it was useless to worship false idols.

Dioscorus was so angry that Barbara had become a Christian that after beating her himself, he turned her over to the authorities, who tortured her and demanded that she give up Christ. She never did, and she died for her Faith. We recognize her as a great saint and martyr of the Church.

Isn't it amazing to think that she made the sign of the cross on a stone building, and it was carved into the stone? St. Barbara had great faith, and the healings at the bathhouse are surely proof that God worked wonders through her.

When we make the sign of the cross, we should always do it with a prayerful and reverent spirit. We are calling down God's blessing on the thing we cross—whether we cross our own bodies or our food.

Here are some good times to make the sign of the cross. You can probably think of more:

» at the beginning and end of a prayer;

» when we enter church and when we leave church;

» every time we hear the words, "the Father, the Son, and the Holy Spirit";

» when we hear the name of the All-Holy Mother of God (Theotokos) or the names of the saints;

» when we are about to hear the Holy Gospel, and after the reading of the Holy Gospel;

» whenever we venerate (kiss) a holy icon, a cross, or the Holy Gospel Book;

» before and after each meal;

» when passing by an accident or when we hear that someone is hurt or sick.

There aren't really any times when you should *not* make the sign of the cross. Make it whenever you are thinking of God and offering a prayer, whether it's big or small.

᪥

How did the earliest Christians make the sign of the cross?

They used one finger to trace the cross on their foreheads or on another object.

What is the significance of the way we hold our fingers when we make the sign of the cross today?

We hold together three fingers for the Trinity, and two for the dual natures of Christ (God and man).

How did St. Barbara learn about God?

St. Barbara witnessed the beauty of nature and understood that God had to be powerful and wonderful. Later, she met some Christian maidens who taught her about Christ and the Holy Trinity.

FOR DISCUSSION: Sometimes a visitor to an Orthodox church gets confused because we don't all cross ourselves at the same times. Many Orthodox people will develop special times when they like to cross themselves—for example, during the Creed, some people cross themselves when we say, "One holy,

catholic, and apostolic Church," because they know that
they are members of the Church, so they cross themselves to
acknowledge that. Is there a special time when you like to cross
yourself that maybe other people would wonder about? Do
you have any special crossing traditions?

The Second Thursday of Great Lent

As we explore the theme of Orthodoxy and the things that make our worship so special, we should consider incense, which we burn in all of our church services and at times of prayer.

You may remember the three Wise Men or Magi who came from the east—a very long journey—to worship the newborn King, our Lord Jesus Christ. On this long journey they brought gifts, including frankincense (which is a type of incense), because Jesus is the High Priest, so it is proper to give Him incense, because priests use incense to honor God's presence.

Incense is a little resin, a mix made of spices and gums, that we can lay on top of a burning charcoal. Priests use a censer to burn the incense as they move around in the church. Did you know that the censer usually has three chains for the Holy Trinity, and twelve little bells for the twelve disciples? As the resin melts and burns away, it releases a fragrant smoke—it both smells and looks beautiful.

In the Book of the Apocalypse (also called Revelation), St. John the Beloved writes, "And the smoke of the incense, with the prayers of the saints, ascended before God from the angel's hand" (Rev. 8:4). We think of our prayers as ascending with the incense—the beautiful scent and the smoke move upward, as if moving toward God, bringing our prayers with them.

In the Vespers services, we always sing, "Lord, I call upon You, hear me. Hear me, O Lord. Let my prayer arise in Your sight as incense. And let the lifting up of my hands be an evening sacrifice. Hear me, O Lord!" We offer incense, and we offer prayers, and together they rise up toward our Lord.

The priest burns incense to represent our prayers, and then he walks around the church and censes things. That means he swings the censer so the fragrant smoke will move toward a specific icon or person; he is censing them by covering them with incense smoke. The priest censes the icons as a way of venerating them, because in them we see the saints and angels who are holy and allow God to work through them. The priest censes the people in the church because each and every one of them has been made in the image of God. We are all icons of Christ, so of course we must be censed too.

When you are censed, you should bow your head, because you are receiving a blessing.

Incense smells beautiful, and God knows that our brains remember things very well with smell. Even when you are very old, the smell of a certain kind of food cooking will probably remind you of your grandmother's kitchen or your favorite restaurant. A powerful smell brings you right back to the place where you smelled it before. So if you go home after church and then smell your clothes, maybe that smell will make you feel like you are back in church. Most importantly, when you walk into church, the scent of incense tells your brain that it's time to pray.

༢

The three wise men brought Jesus incense called frankincense. Why did they bring this to Him?

Incense was an appropriate gift for the high priest, and Jesus Christ is the High Priest.

Incense symbolizes prayer. Why? What do the two have in common?

Just as the fragrant smoke of the incense moves upward toward heaven, so do our prayers.

Why does the priest cense people? What should you do if he censes you?

People are icons of Christ, made in the image and likeness of God, so they are holy. When the priest censes you, you should bow reverently.

FOR DISCUSSION: Incense symbolizes prayer, but it also symbolizes the Holy Spirit. In the Old Testament, God's presence is often connected to a cloud. Do you remember when Moses led his people out of Egypt? They followed a pillar of cloud in the sky that lit up like fire at night. When Moses went up on Mt. Sinai and received the Ten Commandments, the presence of God was a cloud that descended on the mountain the whole time he was there. And when Solomon built the temple for God and they consecrated it (which means that everyone came to the temple to say special prayers to declare it a holy place), a cloud filled every corner of that temple to bless it. At the Transfiguration, when Jesus Christ revealed His glory to some of the disciples, He stood up on Mt. Tabor, and the voice of God spoke from the cloud.

Saint Symeon of Thessalonica writes, "Like a cloud also the incense is offered, symbolizing the Holy Spirit and the transmission of His divine grace and fragrance." So in this way, the clouds of incense smoke call to mind the Holy Spirit and confirm the presence of God.

The Second Friday of Great Lent

A S WE CONSIDER ORTHODOXY AND the things that make our worship so special, today we're thinking about candles—and in particular, about a special miracle that happens every year involving candles.

Pascha is the most glorious feast of the Church, and it's very special everywhere—but at the Church of the Holy Sepulchre in Jerusalem, something amazing happens every year. The Holy Sepulchre is the Tomb of Jesus Christ, the very place where Christ's body was laid and where He resurrected. This is the Tomb that the myrrhbearing women approached, only to find an angel telling them that Christ was gone. When St. Constantine was emperor, he sent his mother, St. Helena, to the Holy Land, and she located the True Cross and the Holy Sepulchre and built a beautiful church. In fact, the one church is large enough to house both the Tomb and the little hill at Golgotha—both Christ's Tomb and the spot where He was crucified have been enclosed inside this beautiful church.

At Pascha, the feast of the Resurrection, many people make the pilgrimage to celebrate in the actual place where the Resurrection happened. Usually, people arrive in the afternoon on Holy Friday and then camp there, waiting for the great miracle that happens every year on Holy Saturday.

On Holy Saturday, at around 11 AM, the Christian Arabs begin chanting loudly. In the thirteenth century, the Turks occupied Jerusalem, and Christians were not allowed to chant in the streets—they had to keep quiet about their Faith and chant only in the churches. Now they exercise the freedom to chant publicly with great joy. They loudly chant traditional hymns while drummers sit on the shoulders of young men who dance vigorously. It's very energetic and exciting. In particular, they love to chant, "We are the Christians, we have been Christians for centuries, and we shall be forever and ever. Amen!"

At 1 PM, the chants quiet down. People become solemn, and silence falls over the gathering, which extends outside the church and up and down the streets—tense, waiting. They expect a great miracle from God, so they pray and prepare themselves and wait.

Every year is the same. A group from the local authorities elbows its way through the crowd. When the Turks occupied Palestine, it was Muslim Turks who pushed through to the front. Today, they are Israelis. They come to represent the Romans at the time of Jesus. The gospels tell us that the Romans went to seal the Tomb of Jesus so that His disciples would not steal his body and say that He had risen. In the same way, today's authorities come on Holy Saturday to seal the Tomb with wax. Before they seal the door, they enter the Tomb and check for any hidden source of fire. When they have confirmed that there is nothing anyone can make fire with inside that Tomb, they seal it closed with the Patriarch of Jerusalem inside (just as Christ was sealed inside so many years ago.) The church is packed tightly with people and is completely dark as they wait.

Patriarch Diodor describes it like this:

I find my way through the darkness towards the inner chamber, in which I fall on my knees. Here I say certain prayers that have been handed down to us through the centuries and, having said them, I wait. Sometimes I may wait a few minutes, but normally the miracle happens immediately after I have said the prayers. From the core of the very stone on which Jesus lay an indefinable light pours forth. It usually has a blue tint, but the colour may change and take many different hues. It cannot be described in human terms. The light rises out of the stone as mist may rise out of a lake—it almost looks as if the stone is covered by a moist cloud, but it is light. This light each year behaves differently. Sometimes it covers just the stone, while other times it gives light to the whole sepulchre, so that people who stand outside the Tomb and look into it will see it filled with light. The light does not burn—I have never had my beard burnt in all the sixteen years I have been Patriarch in Jerusalem and have received the Holy Fire. The light is of a different consistency than normal fire that burns in an oil lamp. . . . At a certain point the light rises and forms a column in which the fire is of a different nature, so that I am able to light my candles from it. When I thus have received the flame on my candles, I go out and give the fire to the Armenian Patriarch and then to the Coptic. (Quote from holyfire.org)

When the door of the Tomb opens, a rumble goes through the crowd, and when they see the light a great cheer goes up. The patriarch emerges and lights the candles of the waiting patriarchs, and then he begins to light the candles of the people—just as your priest does at your church. But with this Holy Fire, something else happens—people are passing the light, but sometimes the fire also begins to jump around the church. It leaps and whirls around and lights the various lamps around the church and even lights the candles of some of the people in different parts of the room.

Right here at the beginning, in the church of the Holy Sepulchre, this first fire is not like regular fire. It is bluish colored, and it does not burn. People put their hands in it and their hands do not burn. Do you remember the burning bush that Moses saw? God was in that bush like a fire, but the bush was not burning up. This Holy Fire is truly of God, for like the fire that glowed in the burning bush, this fire will not burn or damage or consume what enters into it. It burns beautifully and brightly, and it does not burn people's hands if they hold them in the flame. After a while, the fire becomes more like regular fire, loses its bluish color, and burns like earthly fires.

One year, something very remarkable happened with this miracle. In 1579, the Turkish occupiers of Palestine decided that they would not allow the patriarch to enter the Tomb and receive the fire. They locked everything up and refused to allow the usual Christian activities and ceremonies. The crowd of faithful showed up anyway, and they stood in the courtyard all day and into the night. The soldiers would not allow the patriarch in, but he stood there in the courtyard with the people, praying sorrowfully and leaning on a column to the left of the entrance. Night had fallen, and Holy Saturday was ending, and the soldiers did not change their minds: the patriarch had not been allowed inside the church.

Quite suddenly, there was a great, loud sound, and the column beside the patriarch split open as the Holy Fire tore through it. When the patriarch could not come to the fire, the fire came to him. He grabbed for his candle, received this great miracle, and immediately began to pass the fire to the faithful all around him. The courtyard was soon filled with light, and the Turkish soldiers were awestruck. They opened the doors, and the faithful poured into the Church of the Holy Sepulchre to worship with great joy. They entered into the darkened church and began the Pascha liturgy.

Today, those columns still stand outside the entrance to the church, and one of the columns is profoundly cracked. We don't ever fix it, because we hope always to remember this great miracle and the amazing power and love of God.

We Orthodox love to light candles at Pascha and throughout the year. They provide light for our services, but they also remind us of the fire of God. Our God is light and truth—and He comes to us as a fire that burns away sin but does not consume us. When we light candles, we are reminded who our God is. Saint John of Kronstadt wrote in *My Life in Christ*, "When you look at the candles and lamps burning in church, rise in thought from the material fire to the immaterial fire of the Holy Ghost, for our God is a consuming fire."

Our Lord Jesus Christ is the light of the world, and when we receive Holy Communion, we receive that light inside of us. Every time we light a candle and see how it illuminates the darkness, we should remember that the light of Christ within us must also shine before men, that God's Name will be glorified.

꒰

Many people make a pilgrimage to the Church of the Holy Sepulchre in Jerusalem for Holy Saturday and Pascha. Why would they go there in particular?

Because the Holy Sepulchre is the Tomb of Christ, where the Resurrection happened (and because there is a great miracle there every year).

What is the miracle that happens every year?

The Holy Fire: the Patriarch of Jerusalem receives miraculous fire in the Tomb on Holy Saturday.

One year, the patriarch was not allowed into the church or the Tomb for the usual ceremonies. What happened?

God sent the Holy Fire to him, breaking through a pillar and cracking it open. The patriarch received the fire in the courtyard and passed it to all the people.

FOR DISCUSSION: On Pascha, we stand outside and receive the light as we sing, "Christ is risen!" This is the light of Christ, the light of the Resurrection, and we stand in joy and awe as we think about it. Does the wind ever blow your candle out? Do you ever have to re-light it? How? If these candles are symbolic of the spiritual light of Christ that we have received, what would you say about how the world might blow out that light and how we can support one another as a loving community, to help everyone keep shining forth Christ's light into the world?

If you're interested, you can search YouTube for videos of the Holy Fire. It's pretty amazing to watch.

The Second Saturday of Great Lent

AS WE COMPLETE OUR WEEK'S theme of Orthodoxy, we'll consider holy water—and of course, holy water begins with the Baptism of our Lord Jesus Christ on the feast we call Theophany. The story really begins with John the Forerunner (also known as John the Baptist).

John had lived in the desert since he was a young boy. We know him to be the greatest ascetic; he fasted all of his life and had wonderful spiritual and physical discipline. John did not live in the comfort of the cities, like other people, and he didn't eat warm bread fresh from the oven or roasted chicken or lamb like other people. The Scriptures tell us that he lived on honey and wild locusts (fasting year-round) and that he wore itchy camel-hair garments to keep himself from ever being too comfortable.

It was John's job to prepare the way for Jesus, to announce that He was coming and to get the people ready to follow Him. And of course, John himself was ready for that important job, because he had been preparing all of his life for it. He fasted and he prayed, and he focused himself on God. He was prepared when Christ came, and he had baptized many people and told them to repent and to get ready for Christ.

One day, as John stood preaching at the Jordan, Christ Himself walked right up to him. Can you imagine that? John knew who He was right away and said, "Behold, the Lamb of God."

Jesus came to John to be baptized because it was time for Jesus to begin what we call His public ministry, which means that He would gather some disciples and begin teaching and doing miracles.

We are baptized at the beginning of our journey, aren't we? Whether we are baptized as infants or as adults, baptism is what brings us into the life of the Church, making us members ready to receive Holy Communion and all of the blessings of the Church. Christ was also baptized at the beginning of His journey—He had been alive on earth for thirty years, and when He was prepared to begin His public ministry, He was baptized.

But baptism is more than a beginning—it's a cleansing. In baptism, our sins are washed away. But Christ had no sin. His Baptism was different. You and I were sanctified by holy waters; we were washed clean and made holy by the waters of baptism. With Christ, the opposite happened: He sanctified the water—He transformed regular water into something holy and powerful.

Perhaps you have learned about the water cycle, and you know that water evaporates up into the air, then condenses into clouds and dew, and finally precipitates down in the rain and snow. We don't have any new water, because the same water just goes through this cycle again and again. The water we are drinking today is the same water that flooded the earth in Noah's day, it's the same water that parted at the Red Sea for the Israelites to cross, and it's the same water that flowed in the Jordan when Christ was baptized.

All of the water on the earth moves around. The rivers run to the oceans, and the oceans are all connected, and the water gets all mixed around together, both in bodies of water on earth and in the clouds that swirl above us. So when Christ made the water in the Jordan River holy, that water ran to the sea, and it got mixed up with all the other waters—and soon, all of the water carried the blessing of Jesus Christ.

Now something very unusual happened when Christ stepped into the Jordan and was baptized by John: the Jordan River turned around, and the water ran upstream. The mighty river itself felt its Creator's presence, leaped up in joy, and changed direction. You can see in the icon of Christ's Baptism the way the fish move—the water has reversed direction, and the fish are leaping around. Psalm 114 foretells this very moment: verse 3 reads, "The sea saw *it* and fled; Jordan turned back." The Psalms are full of verses about how creation praises the Lord.

Have you ever wondered why we call this event Theophany? This word means "the revelation of God," and we call the feast of Christ's Baptism the Theophany because of what comes next. Matthew wrote in his Gospel that when Jesus was baptized and came up out of the water, the heavens opened up and He saw the Spirit of God, which came down in the form of a dove and landed on Him. After that, a voice from heaven said, "This is My beloved Son, in whom I am well pleased" (Matt. 3:16–17).

At this remarkable moment, as all of the water on earth is sanctified by Christ Himself, Christ emerges from the water, and the heavens open up. The Son stands there in the flesh, the Holy Spirit appears as a dove, and the Father's voice booms down from the heavens, "This is my beloved Son, in whom I am well pleased." The Holy Trinity is all present—Father, Son, and Holy Spirit. As creation leaps for joy, the Holy Trinity reveals itself, and God declares that His beloved Son is good.

When we celebrate the joyous feast of Theophany, we mark the day by asking Christ to bless the waters again. Many priests go to the oceans and the rivers, the bays and the gulfs, and they bless those huge and wonderful bodies of water. And then all of that blessed water mixes with all the other water. Jesus blessed all of the water, and now for thousands of years countless priests have blessed those waters—in a way, it seems that all of the water must be very holy.

On this and a few other feasts, the priests will bless the water, and then they'll walk around the church and bless all of us with the water. And then after Theophany, priests often come to people's houses and bless them. We Orthodox love to spread the blessing of Jesus Christ's love and grace. Often, a family will keep a bottle of holy water in their icon corner, and when someone is sick or worried, they might take a little sip or might wet their finger and trace a cross on their forehead as a way of asking God to bless them as He has blessed that water.

᪗

John the Forerunner's job was to prepare the people for the coming of Christ. What did he do?

He baptized them and told them to repent.

When I was baptized, my sins were cleansed, and I was forgiven. When Jesus was baptized, were His sins forgiven?

Jesus was without sin, so He did not need to be cleansed. Instead, He made the water holy.

Why do we call Jesus' Baptism the Theophany? How did the Trinity show itself?

When Jesus was baptized, we could see the Son of God in the river, and the Holy Spirit came down in the form of a dove, and the voice of the Father called Jesus His "Beloved Son."

FOR DISCUSSION: If John the Forerunner came to you today and told you to repent, that Christ would be here in a moment and you needed to get ready—is there something you would stop doing? Would you stop fighting with your siblings? Would you stop arguing with your parents? What if John were standing before you, in his camel hair coat with his wild hair, and he were telling you to repent, to change your ways? Would you listen? What would you repent of? What sin would you give up? Why not do that today? Who knows when Christ will return—it could be any time. John teaches us to get our house in order before He comes back, and it's excellent advice that we could all take. Why don't we?

The Sunday of St. Gregory Palamas

S T. GREGORY PALAMAS WAS BORN in Constantinople in the
year 1296. His father had died while Gregory was still very
young, so the emperor took an interest in Gregory, who was really
a remarkable child, and helped raise him and educate him. The
boy was very smart and worked hard, so he mastered all the sub-
jects he studied. As he grew up, the emperor hoped that Gregory
would take a position working within his government.

Instead, when he was just twenty years old, Gregory went to Mt.
Athos to become a monk. He wanted to spend all of his energy
praying and learning about God. Gregory's whole family was very
faithful, and his mother and his sisters also became monastics.

Sometimes Gregory had visions—once, the holy Evangelist
John the Theologian appeared to him and promised him his
spiritual protection.

On Mt. Athos, Gregory learned about prayer of the heart,
which is done when one is alone and very quiet and is called *hesychasm* (from the Greek *hesychia*, meaning "calm" and "silence").
Gregory mastered this kind of prayer and became a hesychast (a
person who prays the prayer of the heart).

In the year 1326, because of the threat of Turkish invasions,
Gregory went to Thessalonica, where he was ordained a priest.

He still lived the life of a hermit but also did the work of a priest. Monday through Friday, he was completely alone, in silence and prayer. On weekends, he came out into public to celebrate holy services and to preach his wonderful sermons.

One day, a very well-educated monk named Barlaam, who had written long and wonderful writings on logic and astronomy, came to Mt. Athos and heard about hesychasm, or the prayer of the heart. He said that it was impossible to know the essence of God, and he said that the teachings of the monks about prayer were heresy. *Heresy* is a very serious word meaning "false teachings"—Barlaam was saying that the monks' teachings were against the Church. Barlaam made fun of the monks on Mt. Athos who taught about these methods of prayer and about the uncreated light they had seen in prayer.

St. Gregory, of course, was very well educated, just like Barlaam. They both had studied in the world and were very smart. But St. Gregory had also studied with the monks and understood hesychasm very well, so he was the perfect person to debate this question. He tried to speak with Barlaam at first, to explain the prayer of the heart, but it did not help. He saw that this would not be enough, so he began writing many texts explaining the validity of the prayer of the heart.

The argument between them was about whether we can know God. We can *know about* God, but can we ever *experience* God?

They both agreed that we cannot comprehend the essence of God. We cannot fully understand Him. Think, for example, of all of known space—it is too large for us to grasp. We can see satellite images of space, we can study space, but it's hard for us to really understand just how enormous it is because our brains and our world are so much smaller. And yet, even if we could map all of space and travel every inch of it, this is still only God's creation and is so much smaller than God Himself. Our brains cannot truly comprehend God. We can learn about Him, but we cannot fully grasp Him.

And yet there have been times when human beings have experienced God. Consider the Transfiguration: Jesus took the Apostles Peter, James, and John with Him up on a mountain, and while they were on the mountain, Jesus was transfigured. His face shone like the sun, and His garments became glistening white. He showed them the glory of God, the uncreated light of God, as it shined through Him.

A bright cloud overshadowed them up on that mountain, and a voice came from the cloud saying, "This is my beloved Son, in whom I am well pleased. Hear Him!" (Matt. 17:5). This cloud (which we have seen before in the life of Moses and when Solomon was building the temple) is the Holy Spirit, and this voice can only be the Father.

When the disciples heard God speak, they fell on their faces, filled with awe. They had an amazing experience of the Father, the Son, and the Holy Spirit. Even though God is so much bigger than us, so incomprehensible to us, He showed Himself to the disciples, and they were overwhelmed and amazed and filled with awe.

Jesus came to them and told them to not be afraid. When the three looked up, they saw only Jesus. The experience of seeing God—not just Jesus, but truly experiencing the Holy Trinity—was overwhelming, so Jesus comforted them and helped them recover from it.

When Barlaam and St. Gregory Palamas faced off in a debate at the Constantinople Council of 1341, they stood inside the amazing and enormous church called Hagia Sophia in Constantinople, and they argued about the Transfiguration. St. Gregory argued that God chose to truly reveal Himself to people, to use

His divine energies to show them His glory and His presence. Contrarily, Barlaam argued that this was not really an experience of God; it was some kind of helpful gift from God, but the disciples did not and could not truly experience God Himself.

The council agreed with St. Gregory Palamas: God, who is unapproachable in His essence, reveals Himself through His energies, which are directed toward the world and can be perceived like the light the disciples saw on Mt. Tabor. The council said the teachings of Barlaam were heresy (false teaching), and he fled to Calabria.

Some who agreed with Barlaam continued to argue against St. Gregory, and at one point he was actually locked up in prison for four years. But the next patriarch freed him and named him Archbishop of Thessalonica.

Ultimately, the precious tradition of the prayer of the heart and the true understanding that God reveals Himself in His energies to humans, including the apostles at the Transfiguration and the hesychasts, survived Barlaam's incorrect teachings. The Church remained true to her original teachings, thanks to the voice of St. Gregory Palamas, who would not give up but insisted on defending the truth. Many people say that the Sunday of St. Gregory Palamas is like the Sunday of Orthodoxy Part Two, because it was the next time that Orthodoxy itself was under attack but was ultimately victorious.

In his final years, St. Gregory performed many miracles, healing the sick. The night before he died, St. John Chrysostom appeared to him in a vision. And when he died, his last words were, "To the heights! To the heights!"

༄

What is the prayer of the heart?

This is hesychasm, or very quiet and still prayer. It can also refer to the Jesus Prayer.

During the years when he was a priest, how did St. Gregory find time alone for solitary prayer?

He spent five days a week completely alone, in silence and prayer, and came to his people on the weekends only to celebrate holy services and to preach sermons.

St. Gregory debated Barlaam about whether or not people could really experience God. Who did the Church agree with?

The Church ultimately agreed with St. Gregory Palamas's position that people can experience God's energies, as Moses did and as the apostles did at the Transfiguration.

FOR DISCUSSION: Talk about times when you have experienced God.

The Third Monday of Great Lent

B ECAUSE OUR WEEK BEGAN WITH St. Gregory Palamas, who helped us to better understand how God reveals Himself to us, and who defended the great tradition of hesychasm (prayer of the heart), this week we will focus on prayer.

In the Gospel of Matthew, we find that Jesus specifically explained how we should pray:

And when you pray, you shall not be like the hypocrites. For they love to pray standing in the synagogues and on the corners of the streets, that they may be seen by men. Assuredly, I say to you, they have their reward. (Matt. 6:5)

First, Jesus tells us what not to do: don't put on a show so that everyone else will think that you're so great at praying. Don't try to make everyone see you praying so that they'll think you're holy. Jesus says that people who show off their prayers "have their reward." That means they are only trying to get attention, and that works. But if what you really want is a different reward—like growing closer to God—you'll have to pray a different way:

But you, when you pray, go into your room, and when you have shut your door, pray to your Father who is in the secret place; and your Father who sees in secret will reward you openly. (Matt. 6:6)

Jesus wants us to pray humbly and quietly, without drawing attention to ourselves. This can be done in our own rooms—and really, there is a way that you can pray humbly in church too. When we pray in church, we don't yell or draw attention to ourselves. Instead, we stand quietly and peacefully, our words are mere whispers, and our heads are often down. We pray with humility, without drawing attention to ourselves.

And when you pray, do not use vain repetitions as the heathen do. For they think that they will be heard for their many words. Therefore do not be like them. For your Father knows the things you have need of before you ask Him. (Matt. 6:7–8)

Sometimes people think that saying "do not use vain repetitions" means that we should not repeat prayers that we have memorized, but you'll see that Jesus is about to offer us the Lord's Prayer to memorize and repeat, so that cannot be what He means. Instead, Jesus is teaching us that we should not try to invent long, fancy prayers that don't mean anything just to impress people. Instead, we should offer prayers that are meaningful and real. When you pray humbly and you really mean what you are saying, even if you are reading from a prayer book, you are being sincere and real, and not trying to impress God with your words.

Finally, Jesus tells us that our Father "knows the things you have need of before you ask Him." We should not lecture God about what we need—He knows what we really need, and we should just ask Him to take care of us in His wisdom.

Jesus teaches us to pray like this instead:

Our Father who art in heaven, hallowed be Thy name. Thy kingdom come. Thy will be done on earth as it is in heaven. Give us this day our daily bread. And forgive us our trespasses, as we forgive those who trespass against us. And lead

us not into temptation, but deliver us from the evil one. For Thine is the king-
dom and the power and the glory forever. Amen. (Matt. 6:9–13)

We begin with "Our Father." Jesus could have told us to say "My
Father," which is beautiful, because it reminds us that He has
made us adopted sons and daughters of God. But he says "Our
Father," because this shows both that we are sons and daughters
and that we pray together, as a community.

Hallowed means "holy," so when we say, "Hallowed be Thy
name," we are observing that God's name is holy, which it is. We
could also ask ourselves, *Is God's name holy when I say it? Do I shine with His*
light, so that when I speak of God, others can sense His holiness?

We continue with, "Thy kingdom come. Thy will be done on
earth as it is in heaven." This line observes that Christ will return
someday and the Kingdom of heaven will be on earth. But it's
more than that—when we say, "Thy Kingdom come," we are inviting the Kingdom in. In the original Greek, this is an invitation,
like "Come, dear Kingdom!" We are inviting the Lord to reign
over us, asking to be made His servants. More than simply recog-
nizing that the Kingdom will be here eventually, we are asking to
become a part of the Kingdom today.

Jesus tells us to pray, "Give us this day our daily bread." Our
daily bread is the food that we eat which sustains us physically, but
it is also the bread that nourishes us spiritually. We receive this
bread at Holy Communion, and we know that Jesus is the Bread
of Life. We bring both our physical hunger and our spiritual
hunger to God.

"And forgive us our trespasses, as we forgive those who trespass
against us." As we discussed during the first week of Lent, God
has forgiven each of us so much, and if we cannot learn from that
experience and feel merciful and forgiving to others, then the

mercies we have received will fade away. Like the unforgiving servant, if we aren't forgiving, we cannot receive forgiveness. Somehow, our hearts are only open to forgiveness when we can humbly pass along forgiveness too.

The last line Jesus gives us reads, "And lead us not into temptation, but deliver us from the evil one." It's not that God leads us to temptation, but that we hope He will lead us away, for we recognize our weakness. Temptation can come from outside us, if someone else tries to talk us into doing the wrong thing. Temptation can come from within our own hearts as well. Our weaknesses are our temptations, and in humility, we ask that God shield us and protect us, for we know that alone we are not strong enough to overcome all temptation. But through Christ there is nothing we cannot do.

Have you ever noticed how all of our prayers end with "amen"? That means "so be it" or "let it be so." It's like sealing the prayer with one final request that the prayer may be granted.

We are lucky indeed to find that our Lord gave us specific instructions on how to pray. If you'd like to look this up in your Bible, today's reading is from Matthew 6:5-14.

॰॰

Does Jesus want us to pray in front of everyone else, making sure that they see?

No, Jesus teaches us not to make a show of our prayers, but to be quiet and humble.

What do we mean when we say, "Thy kingdom come. Thy will be done on earth as it is in heaven"?

We are saying that Christ will return and establish His Kingdom over the earth as it is in heaven, but we are also inviting Christ's Kingdom and God's will into our lives today.

What do we mean by, "Give us this day our daily bread"?

We need to be nourished physically and spiritually, so we are asking God to help us be fed with bread (and other food) and also to be fed spiritually, as He is the Bread of Life.

FOR DISCUSSION: What do you think is the most interesting part of the Lord's Prayer?

The Third Tuesday of Great Lent

HAVE YOU EVER ASKED YOURSELF, *What exactly happens when I pray?*

When we think about Adam and Eve in the Garden of Eden, before they ate the fruit of the tree of the knowledge of good and evil, they would walk in the garden, and it seems that God would walk with them. They could talk with God—really talk with Him and hear His answers.

Prayer is our opportunity to do the same thing—to spend some time with God. Praying really is like talking to God, but we don't hear His answers the way Adam and Eve used to hear Him. If I talk to my friend by saying words, usually my friend answers back with words. God is different. He does send us answers, but not necessarily with words, as people do.

In the Holy Scriptures, God speaks to his people, Israel. He says, "I shall give you a new heart and put a new spirit within you; I shall take the heart of stone out of your flesh and give you a heart of flesh" (Ezek. 36:26). He is really speaking to all of us, because we all have hard hearts of unfeeling stone sometimes, but God can make them living, soft hearts of flesh.

Our bodies have hearts, and so do our souls. Our body's heart beats, and it pumps blood to all of our organs. But what about our soul's heart? Have you ever seen a person act hard-heartedly toward another person? Maybe he pushed someone down on the ground and laughed, or maybe she teased someone mercilessly. People who show no compassion or sympathy for the pain they cause are often called hard-hearted. But on the other hand, others have softer hearts that can be hurt easily and also hurt when they see other people in pain. God wants us to have soft hearts that love our neighbors, mourn with the sad, and celebrate with the joyful.

All of the tools that God gives us (prayer, fasting, attending church services, charity and service work, and study) are designed to transform us. God wants to shape us into the people He created us to be. In particular, through prayer He can change our hearts. As we spend more and more time in the presence of God, He transforms our hearts from stone to flesh—from hard to soft.

Imagine if you were to take a piece of clay and rub it in your warm hands. The clay begins hard and almost solid and impenetrable, like our hearts, but as we work it with our warm hands, the clay becomes soft and flexible. God's warm presence does that for us; He transforms the hardness of our hearts into softness. And just like that clay, our hearts might just grow hard again if we stop praying for a while, but simply returning to prayer begins to warm us up again.

We began this week with St. Gregory Palamas, who once gave a sermon on the Publican and the Pharisee, which is a parable Jesus told us. A Pharisee went proudly to pray and said, "Thank you, God, that I am not like this other man!" Next to him stood the publican, a tax collector, someone who probably did a lot of bad things. The Pharisee didn't feel sorry for the sad publican, who was on the floor praying, prostrated in his repentance—he just felt proud that he was so much better than him. The publican, though he was a bad man, prayed humbly, "Lord, have mercy on me, a sinner!" Jesus preferred the publican's prayer to the Pharisee's prayer.

Saint Gregory Palamas said, "Faith and contrition make prayer and supplication for the remission of sins effective, once evil deeds have been renounced, but despair and hardness of heart make it ineffectual." That basically means that the publican's prayer showed faith in God and contrition, or a sadness for his sins, and therefore his sins were forgiven. On the other hand, the Pharisee's hardness of heart, his pride and lack of concern for others, made it impossible for his sins to be forgiven.

Praying with a soft, humble, and loving heart brings us closer to God, while praying with a hard, cold heart does not. A soft heart loves more, feels more, and, most importantly, is more able to receive God's love and His mercy and His messages. If we want to walk in the garden with God, we need soft hearts so that those hearts can feel the messages that God sends.

We know that God is love, and that soft hearts feel love intensely—so when we allow Him to make our hearts soft, we can feel His presence more intensely. That's why we pray, why we worship, and why we participate in the life of the Church: we spend time in the presence of God in order to soften our hearts, that we might feel His presence and live in His love.

ॐ

Did Adam and Eve communicate with God in the garden? How?

They walked with Him and talked—and He answered.

What is the difference between a hard heart and a soft one?

A hard heart is unfeeling and uncaring, while a soft heart is compassionate and loving—and can better feel God's presence.

What kinds of activities help us soften our hearts?

Prayer and church services, fasting, almsgiving, and more.

FOR DISCUSSION: Can you think of an example (from a book or a movie or from your own real life) of a person who acts as if they have a hard heart? How about a soft heart? Have you ever felt yourself having a hard heart or a soft heart? What is it like when your heart is soft?

The Third Wednesday of Great Lent

THE PRAYERS OF THE CHURCH can teach us at the same time that they're helping us to express ourselves. For instance, consider this prayer we say upon entering a church:

> *I will come into Your house in the greatness of Your mercy: and in fear I will worship toward Your holy temple. Lead me, O Lord, in Your righteousness because of my enemies; make Your way straight before me, that with a clear mind I may glorify You forever, One Divine Power worshiped in three persons: Father, Son, and Holy Spirit. Amen.*

When we walk into church from the busy world outside, this prayer helps change our mood and the way we are thinking as we enter into this holy space. Maybe we were running late and rushing around, maybe we've been arguing with each other or listening to loud music and laughing. We've been in a non-church mood, and it's time to transition into a worshipful attitude. This prayer takes our minds and firmly places them in the church we enter. As we whisper the words "In fear I will worship toward Your holy temple. Lead me, O Lord," we redirect our minds, calling us to awe and fear as we dare to enter this holy place. This prayer calls our brains to worship. The words form us into something fit for church, clearing our minds and moving them into position to receive God's grace and His mercy.

Prayers teach us; they lead us into the most useful way of think-ing about our situation. If they were simply expressing thoughts we already had, they couldn't move us to better places. It's a bless-ing to pray a prayer that stretches us and forms us into saints.

The prayers before we receive Holy Communion are very long and beautiful, and sometimes the words can be confusing. But when we understand and think about the simple ideas they are teaching us, we can learn so much about preparing our hearts to receive Jesus Christ. For example, here is one pre-Communion prayer written by St. John Chrysostom:

> *O Lord my God, I know that I am not worthy nor sufficient that You should enter under my roof into the habitation of my soul, for it is all deserted and in ruins, and You have no fitting place in me to lay Your head. But as from the heights of Your glory You did humble Yourself, so now bear me in my humility; as You did deign to lie in a manger in a cave, so deign now also to come into the manger of my mute soul and corrupt body. As You did not refrain from entering into the house of Simon the leper, or shrink from eating there with sinners, so also vouchsafe to enter the house of my poor soul, all leprous and full of sin.*

Just before receiving Holy Communion, we pray about preparing our soul as a habitation for our Lord. A habitation is like a hab-itat—it's a home. When we receive Holy Communion, we receive Jesus Christ so that He can live inside of us. That means that our soul is a home for Him to live in. We can try to picture a little house inside of us—maybe it looks like a regular house, or like a cottage or a castle. You could spend some time imagining yours if you like—you could even draw it and think about how it should be.

If this house is our spiritual heart, then we can imagine that its condition reflects our spiritual life. Every time we are praying, we're in the house, and it's getting clean and cozy. Every time we go to confession, it's as if the house is cleaned until it is spotless.

The sacraments, study, prayer, and fasting—these things all make our house sweet and clean. But if we are not praying, if we go for long stretches without opening up our spiritual homes by attending church and reading the Scriptures and reaching out to help people, then our houses are closed and shuttered, filled with cobwebs and dust and dirt. If we're really abandoning the Christian life, they can begin to look like ruins. And if we are sinful and we are hurting people, we are adding more dirt to our spiritual houses. But when we come back to Christ we can clean them up and bring them back to life. He will even come inside our spiritual hearts and help us revive them.

When we receive Holy Communion, we are truly receiving the Lord, inviting him to come and abide in us. Saint John Chrysostom is so wise to ask whether we have a good home for Him in our hearts. Every time we come to liturgy, we should ask ourselves, *What is the condition of my heart today? Is it dirty and dusty and not ready for our Lord?* We pray, "Bear me in my humility; as You did deign to lie in a manger in a cave, so deign now also to come into the manger of my mute soul and corrupt body." Christ was born in a manger. He is humble and does not require a palace. He is willing to come into our dirty, sad hearts and to help us bring them back to the beauty that God intended for us. With Christ, the Light of the World, in our hearts, they will surely shine brightly.

This is a beautiful prayer to pray the night before receiving Holy Communion and to repeat as we stand in line to receive. Whether we memorize it perfectly or just think about the idea of it, it's a blessing as we prepare our hearts to receive our Lord.

The prayers right before Holy Communion end with a reference to two people who knew Jesus Christ but who behaved very differently at the time of His death: Judas Iscariot and the repentant thief, also known as the good thief on the cross, or St. Dismas. Both men knew Christ and recognized that He was the Son of God, but while Judas gave Him a kiss to betray Him, the thief humbly asked Him to remember him in His Kingdom. The prayer reads,

> *Receive me today, Son of God, as a partaker of Your mystical Supper. I will not reveal Your mystery to Your adversaries. Nor will I give You a kiss as did Judas. But as the thief I confess to You: Lord, remember me in Your kingdom.*

As we approach the chalice, our last prayer is a promise: I will not betray my Lord, but instead, let me be like that good thief on the cross. The good thief had lived a life of sin, but at the last moment, he looked upon our Lord Jesus Christ and repented. He recognized Christ's goodness and His divinity. We are not perfect, and we will not lead perfect lives, but we hope that like that good thief, we will always be wise enough to repent and to ask for Jesus Christ's mercy on us. Just as Jesus told the good thief, "I will see you in Paradise," we hope that He will have mercy on us too.

Our prayers teach us to be humble: we picture ourselves as the thief on the cross just as we approach for Holy Communion. May we always approach our Lord with humility and faith and love!

༂

How can prayers teach us?

Prayers show us what we should be thinking and help us to ease ourselves into the right frame of mind for the situation (focusing as we enter church, preparing for communion, etc.).

If we picture a home for Jesus in our hearts, what would make that little home dirty?

Whenever we are not using our spiritual hearts by praying, attending services, studying the Scriptures, etc., then our little homes are like an abandoned cabin in the woods: they get dirty and dusty, and eventually things begin to break and fall apart. If we are doing bad things such as hurting people, then that builds up dirt in our little homes.

What makes that home clean and beautiful?

Prayer, study, and fasting all help us clean up our little spiritual home. And Jesus coming inside us through Holy Communion will make it cleaner too. Confession can really make it shine.

Why is it good for us to think of ourselves as the good thief on the cross?

He was sinful, as we are, but he repented and asked for God's mercy—and God gave it to him. We hope that He will have mercy on us, too.

FOR DISCUSSION: Can you think of any other prayers that help you get your mind into the right place? Do you have other prayers that teach you? And how do you picture the home for Jesus in your own heart?

The Third Thursday of Great Lent

A S WE CONSIDER PRAYER, WE find in the Scriptures many faithful people who were asked to pray to a false god but would not. They prayed only to the One True God, the Holy Trinity. For instance, let's consider the three holy youths who were taken to Babylon but did not forget God, even in a strange land. (You'll find this story in the Book of Daniel, chapter 3).

The three young men, who were friends of the Prophet Daniel, were smart and well educated, and they held good positions in the government. Their Hebrew names were Hananiah, Mishael, and Azariah. They were also given Babylonian names—Shadrach, Meshach, and Abednego—so sometimes you will hear them called by different names.

King Nebuchadnezzar had an enormous golden statue built of himself, and on the day it was dedicated, his herald announced a new law. He cried out in a loud voice, "Whenever you hear the sound of the trumpet, pipe, harp, four-stringed instrument, psaltery, symphony, and every kind of music there is, you must drop down to your knees to worship the golden statue. Anyone who does not fall down and worship will be thrown into the burning fiery furnace."

This law was a problem for the three young men and for Daniel, because they worshiped only the one true God, the Holy

Trinity. They could not bow down and worship this statue, no matter how many laws were made.

So sometimes the people would hear the sound of the trumpet, pipe, harp, four-stringed instrument, psaltery, symphony, and every kind of music, and then they would all bow down and worship the golden statue.

But some people knew that the three youths would not worship that statue, and they went to the king and said that Hananiah, Mishael, and Azariah were not worshiping with everyone else.

So Nebuchadnezzar asked them, "Is it true that you do not follow my law? Do you really not serve my gods or worship the statue? Now then, if you are ready you should worship the statue. But if you will not worship it, you will be thrown into the burning fiery furnace. Then what god will save you?"

Hananiah, Mishael, and Azariah did not even consider worshiping that statue. They knew that they did indeed worship a God who was more powerful than King Nebuchadnezzar.

They said, "We will not answer you about this statue. There is a God in heaven, whom we serve, and He will save us from the burning fiery furnace. He will deliver us from your hands, O king. We will not serve your gods, nor will we worship your statue."

As you can imagine, Nebuchadnezzar was very angry at their response. He commanded his men to heat the furnace seven times more, until it burned as hot as it could burn. Then his men tied the three young men tightly with ropes and threw them into the burning fiery furnace, expecting them to burn up and die for dishonoring Nebuchadnezzar.

But something amazing happened. The flames did not hurt them. The fire burned the ropes that were tied around them. They were praying, singing, and praising God. They danced in the middle of the flames, praising the Lord.

Now the king's servants kept adding fuel to the furnace to make it hotter and hotter. The flames were so high that they shot forty-nine cubits above the furnace. That's more than seventy-three feet high. The flames broke out of the furnace and began to burn the area around it.

In all of this terribly hot and enormous fire, Azariah and his companions were still okay. The Angel of the Lord went down into the furnace and joined them. He made the inside of the furnace feel so comfortable—it was as if a cool breeze were blowing through it. The fire did not hurt them.

God heard their prayers and protected them from the fiery furnace, and He was with them—He sent them company in their difficulties, answering their prayers.

Now Nebuchadnezzar heard their singing and asked, "Didn't we cast three men, all bound in ropes, into the fire? . . . Behold, I see four men! They are untied and they're walking in the midst of the fire. The fourth one looks like the Son of God."

There in the furnace, the three youths sang a beautiful thanksgiving prayer, blessing the Lord and thanking Him for taking such good care of them. God heard them and came to them in their time of need, so they were very grateful.

Then the king approached the door of the burning fiery furnace, and called out: "Servants of the Most High God, come here!" All three youths came out of the fire, and everyone saw that they had not been harmed at all. Even their clothes were not burned, and they didn't smell like smoke. It was as if they had never been in that furnace.

King Nebuchadnezzar, seeing how their God had protected them and come to dance with them in their victory, said, "Blessed is their God, who sent His Angel and saved His servants who trusted in Him!"

ॐ

How did the people know when they were supposed to fall down and worship the statue?

Whenever they heard the sound of the trumpet, pipe, harp, four-stringed instrument, psaltery, symphony, and every kind of music there was, that was their cue to fall down to their knees to worship the golden statue.

Why couldn't the three youths worship the statue?

Because there is only one true God, and we worship only Him.

When the king's men threw them into the burning fiery furnace, what happened?

The fire did not harm them at all. It burned up the ropes, freeing them to dance and praise God. Azariah prayed, and the Angel of the Lord came into the furnace and made it feel as if it wasn't even hot in there.

What did Nebuchadnezzar think when he saw the four figures in the furnace?

He knew it was a miracle, and he recognized the fourth as the Son of God. He admitted that their Most High God had saved them.

FOR DISCUSSION: God hears our prayers. What's more, He comes to us in our suffering. The Son of God did not abandon His beloved youths in this strange land filled with false gods, but when they were cast into the terrible fiery furnace, He joined them there. He loved them so much that He would go anywhere to protect them. Especially when someone is suffering, God comes to them, joining them in the difficult places. People often feel God's presence when they pray during difficult times. Can you think of an example?

The Third Friday of Great Lent

TODAY, WE'RE THINKING ABOUT HOW to persist in prayer, how to keep praying when it feels as if we should stop.

Sometimes God answers our prayers right away; we feel as if He heard us and said, "Yes!" But there are times when we pray and it just doesn't feel as if God is hearing us. We pray and pray about something, and nothing happens. Maybe that silence is an answer. Maybe God's answer is, "Wait a little while," or maybe it's just, "No, that's not for the best."

When this happens, we should stop and ask ourselves, why are we praying about this thing? Are we praying selfishly? Are we really trusting God and praying that He will do His holy will? If we are praying selfishly because we just want something to happen, we need to change our prayer. We should begin to pray that God will change our hearts so that we can accept His will, instead of continually praying for the thing that seems so important to us.

Elder Barsanuphius of Optina once told a story that shows us one way to change our prayer. He told about a visit he had from one of the monks in his monastery. The monk said, "Abba, I am so discouraged. I don't think I am changing for the better. I still feel weak and sinful, even though I keep praying and living as a monk."

The elder said, "If God just judges us based on what we do, He will not find anything good in us."

The monk asked, "Well, then, how can I ever have hope to be saved?"

The elder answered, "There is always hope. Always say the Jesus Prayer, and then trust God's will completely."

"But what if my mind and my heart aren't always paying attention when I pray the Jesus Prayer?" asked the monk.

The elder answered, "The Jesus Prayer is very strong. The powers of the enemy run from people who pray this prayer. Some pray it better than others, but everyone who prays it will find that God is saving them."

"I have been resurrected!" the monk exclaimed. "I won't feel so discouraged anymore."

We should remember Elder Barsanuphius's wise advice: "Always say the Jesus Prayer, and leave everything to the will of God."

But what if we are trusting God completely, praying that He does His holy will, and we still don't sense any kind of answer? Sometimes, God may be using this to see if we will persevere or if we will quit in our prayer.

There is a beautiful story in the holy gospels: one day Jesus and His disciples arrived in the region of Tyre and Sidon. A woman from Canaan was there, and she began to cry out, "Have mercy on me, O Lord, Son of David! My daughter is possessed by a demon!" (You can find this story in Matthew 15:21–28.)

Jesus did not answer the woman. She kept on asking and asking Him for mercy and help. The disciples finally came to Jesus and asked Him to please send this woman away, because she kept bothering them. Jesus answered, "I was sent to help the Jewish people." He meant that because she was a Canaanite, not a Hebrew Jew, He was not sent to help her.

The woman did not quit asking. Instead, she came very respectfully before Jesus Himself and said, "Lord, help me!"

Jesus answered her in a parable kind of way. He said, "It's not good to take the children's bread and give it to the little dogs." Jesus was not calling the woman a dog, but He was saying that He would not take the healing—which was life-giving, just like bread—away from God's children, the Hebrews, and give it instead to a Canaanite.

The woman was so sure that He could heal her daughter, and she was so hopeful that He would, that she answered back, also in a parable kind of way. She said, "Yes, Lord, but the little dogs get to eat the crumbs that fall from their master's table." She was not calling herself a dog, either; she was just using our Lord's example to show Him that she had so much faith that He could heal her daughter, that even if He gave the daughter a crumb of His healing, she would be healed.

Jesus then answered the woman and said, "You have great faith. May your daughter be healed, just as you have asked." And the daughter was healed right then.

The woman in this story did not quit praying. Her heart was in the right place: she knew that Jesus is God, and she had faith that He had the power to heal her daughter. She was asking for her daughter, not for herself. St. John Chrysostom says that Jesus waited to heal her daughter to allow her to demonstrate her virtues for His disciples, who were annoyed by her and who would not expect to admire the faith of a Canaanite woman. By continuing to ask, she showed persistence and her great faith, and by accepting her place below the chosen people of God, she showed great humility. Jesus was not being unkind but was intentionally allowing her goodness to be revealed.

Another thing to think about with our prayers is whether they are fervent, which means "intense" and "passionate." St. Nikolai Velimirovich said,

Prayer consisting of words alone does not help if the heart does not participate in prayer. God hears only a fervent prayer. Abba Zoilus of Thebaid was once returning from Mt. Sinai and met a monk who complained to him that they were suffering much from drought in the monastery. Zoilus said to him: "Why don't you pray and beg God?" The monk replied: "We have prayed and have begged, but there is no rain." To this, Zoilus replied: "It is evident that you are not praying fervently. Do you want to be convinced that it is so?" Having said this, the elder raised his hands to heaven and prayed. Abundant rain fell to the earth. Seeing this, the astonished monk fell to the ground and bowed before the elder, but the elder, fearing the glory of men, quickly fled. The Lord Himself said: "Ask and it will be given you" (St. Luke 11:9). In vain are mouths full of prayer if the heart is empty. God does not stand and listen to the mouth but to the heart. Let the heart be filled with prayer even though the mouth might be silent. God will hear and will receive the prayer. For God only listens to a fervent prayer.

When we find ourselves praying but getting no answer from God, let us stop and consider. First, let's examine our hearts and see if we are praying selfishly, or if we really trust God to do His holy will; let's try to pray the Jesus Prayer and trust Him to do what is best in the situation. Let's be persistent and faithful, trusting that the Lord can accomplish what we need Him to do. Let's ask ourselves if we really mean our prayers—are we truly praying from the heart?

And finally, perhaps one of the best prayers for those times when prayer is difficult comes directly from the Scriptures: a man who has come to Jesus for the healing of his son calls out to Him, "Lord, I believe! Help my unbelief!" (Mark 9:24). He does have faith, and he does believe—but there is also some last part of him, some corner of his heart where unbelief lives, and that is true for all of us sometimes. So in those cases where it's hard to want God's will or to be patient and await an answer, and where the long wait sometimes makes us wonder if God is even listening, we can cry out with him, "Lord, I believe. Help my unbelief!"

⌇

What might God be saying if we do not get an answer to a prayer?

"Wait a little, not yet," or maybe "No, this is not what is best right now."

When the monk did not feel as if his monastic life and prayers were helping him to be closer to God, what did Elder Barsanuphius tell him to do?

The Elder told him to change his prayer. He said that the monk should pray the Jesus Prayer and trust that God will do His holy will, and that he would be changed for the better.

How did the woman from Canaan pray?

She called out to Jesus again and again. She said, "Have mercy on me, O Lord, Son of David! My daughter is possessed by a demon!" and "Lord, help me!"

Did the Canaanite woman have faith that Jesus could heal her daughter? How do you know?

She had great faith, which she showed when she kept asking and asking and would not stop. Also, she told Him that even a crumb of His healing would be enough for her daughter.

For Discussion: The monk was living a life apart from the world so that he could pray and get closer to God, but he still did not feel as if God was answering his prayers. The Canaanite woman did not know all the proper prayers to use to ask God for healing, and she was not one of God's chosen people,

so she would not have been part of any of their worship services that could have helped her learn one. But both of them
can help us learn how to pray. Which one of these two people
helped *you* learn to pray better today?

The Third Saturday of Great Lent

W E FINISH OUR WEEK ON prayer with one of the most beautiful prayers of the twentieth century, the akathist hymn titled "Glory to God for All Things."

The title comes from the last words spoken by St. John Chrysostom. He was the Patriarch of Constantinople and was well loved by the people. As you probably know, he was renowned for being a great speaker, and he is quoted frequently even now, more than one thousand years later. Saint John Chrysostom is responsible for the liturgy we use in church today. Though we know him to be a great saint and a Church Father, when he was patriarch many people were upset with his teachings (because he preached against the rich who were not merciful to the poor). In fact, they removed him from his position as patriarch and forced him to leave Constantinople. He did such wonderful service for the Church and taught the people so much, and yet he died far away from them—and he was not bitter. His last words were "Glory to God for all things!" It is truly admirable that a person can be grateful to God during bad times and even grateful for bad things. It makes us think of Christ on the Cross, because He said, "Forgive them, Father, for they know not what they do." If we wish to be like Christ, then even in the midst of suffering we must have a loving and forgiving heart.

Metropolitan Tryphon Turkestanov wrote a beautiful Akathist

filled with praise and thanksgiving in a time of pain and struggle and gave it this name from St. John Chrysostom.

Metropolitan Tryphon was born with a different name: Prince Boris Petrovich Turkestanov. His parents were noble people in Russia. Little Boris was sickly as an infant, but his mother, who loved to pray in the church of the Holy Martyr Tryphon, made a vow to the holy martyr that if the child got well, she would dedicate him to God. Soon, Boris's health improved, and he was very well. His mother was so relieved! His mother was so grateful for the intercessions of the Holy Martyr Tryphon.

His pious mother also took the child to Optina Monastery to receive a blessing from Elder Ambrose. When the elder saw the mother and son approaching, he told all the other visitors to "make way for the bishop," even though Boris was still a very young child.

After he finished school, Boris became a monk at that same monastery under the same Elder Ambrose. He was tonsured with a new name, Tryphon, after the martyr to whom his mother had dedicated him as a child. Over the years, he became a priest and then—as the elder had once predicted—a bishop.

As bishop, Tryphon went to the front during World War I, where his health became very bad—so bad that he could not fulfill his duties as bishop and was granted a release. Though he was not physically well enough to work, he was raised to the rank of archbishop in 1923 and metropolitan in 1931. Soon thereafter, he lost his sight and spent his final years blind and with much physical suffering.

In addition to his own very bad health, Metropolitan Tryphon lived through terrible times. During these years, Russia was under the Soviet Union, and these were difficult and sad times for the Church. The Soviet state attempted to destroy religion completely and attacked the Church in many different ways. Christians were persecuted, tortured, and killed. Ultimately, millions died—numbers much higher than the persecutions in the early Church.

During his last years, blinded, sick, and dying, the metropolitan wrote an akathist of thanksgiving called "Glory to God for All Things," in which he thanks God for everything—even the bad things surrounding him. Metropolitan Tryphon died on June 14, 1934, and many people still visit his grave today.

The akathist was found among the belongings of Fr. Gregory Petrov when he died in a Soviet prison camp in 1940. This song of praise amidst the most terrible suffering must have been precious to him, and through him many Orthodox people have discovered and loved this beautiful prayer.

Every day, both good and bad things come to us. We'll hear distressing news, worry for our loved ones, and find ourselves disappointed or pained in some way every day. The best way to respond is with prayer and thanksgiving. Let us trust in God and give Him thanks! Here is a small sample of this beautiful akathist:

Glory to God for All Things: An Akathist of Thanksgiving

KONTAKION 8

How near You are in the day of sickness. You Yourself visit the sick; You Yourself bend over the sufferer's bed. His heart speaks to You. In the throes of sorrow and suffering You bring peace and unexpected consolation. You are the comforter. You are the love that watches over and heals us. To You we sing the song: Alleluia!

IKOS 8

When in childhood I called upon You consciously for the first time, You heard my prayer, and You filled my heart with the blessing of peace. At that moment I knew Your goodness and knew how blessed are those who turn to You. I started to call upon You night and day; and now, even now, I call upon Your name.

Glory to You, who satisfy my desires with good things!

Glory to You, who watch over me day and night!

Glory to You, who cure affliction and emptiness with the healing flow of time!

Glory to You, for no loss is irreparable in You, Giver of eternal life to all!

Glory to You, who make immortal all that is lofty and good!

Glory to You, who promise us the longed-for meeting with our loved ones who have died!

Glory to You, O God, from age to age!

No matter what comes our way—whether we have an easy day or a really difficult day, let us remember St. John Chrysostom's words and Bishop Tryphon's prayer of gratitude. They will help us to pray, "Glory to God for all things!"

⌇

Saint John Chrysostom had been Patriarch of Constantinople, but he was removed from his throne and kept away from his city when he died. What were his last words?

Glory to God for all things!

When Prince Boris became a monk, he received a new name. Why did they choose that name?

They used the name of St. Tryphon the Martyr because he healed Boris when he was young.

Prince Boris lived with much sickness in his life, but what was the other kind of suffering going on?

In Soviet Russia, the Church was terribly persecuted. Christians were tortured and killed.

FOR DISCUSSION: Why is it so important to give thanks and praise even when things are bad? Can you think of times when you were struggling or things seemed bad? Would it make things better or worse for you to praise God and give thanks? Why?

The Sunday of the Holy Cross

TODAY IS THE SUNDAY OF the Holy Cross: we celebrate Christ's Holy Cross here in the midst of Great Lent, preparing us for the commemoration of the Crucifixion on Holy Friday and reminding us that Great Lent is a period when we are crucified with Christ.

What does it mean to be crucified with Christ?

During Great Lent, we are working hard to cut off those sinful habits we have developed. When we fast from food, we are training ourselves to be obedient and also to think of food as fuel for our bodies rather than to rely on it for comfort or happiness. (Have you ever had a bad day and thought that eating comfort foods or desserts would make you feel better? We often look for emotional support from food, but it's just food. We should turn to God and to the people He has put in our lives, because God and families and friends love us, but food cannot love us back.)

During Lent, we might also try to break other bad habits. If we find that we spend too much time playing video games or are becoming addicted to television, this is a good time to stop doing those things or to limit ourselves, to help us break free from those things that become bad habits and steal too much of our time and energy.

We also try to break from other sinful behaviors, like fighting with people instead of listening to their point of view and trying to work out problems, or complaining, gossiping, or talking about people behind their backs. We spend these special weeks trying to be the best Orthodox Christians we can be, and that means that we are trying destroy our sinful habits. That is part of what we mean by "crucified with Christ"—we want to crucify or kill off our sinful habits.

Halfway through the great fast, the Church shows us the precious and life-giving Cross to refresh our souls. We are reminded why we are doing this. The Cross reminds us how our Lord suffered for us. He was completely innocent and without sin, and yet He allowed Himself to be beaten and spat upon and hung on a cross to die a painful death. We have been struggling to fast, and now we are reminded of Christ's example. We are not the first to struggle, and our struggle is nothing compared to His. The Cross reminds us that through pain and suffering we shall see the fulfillment of our hopes: the heavenly inheritance and eternal glory.

In a sense, we can think of ourselves as preparing to receive our Lord Jesus Christ, the King of kings, at Pascha. Imagine how a king arrives: his royal standards and flags, his trophies, and all the emblems and symbols of his victory come in a procession, and then the king himself appears in the triumphant parade. The Sunday of the Holy Cross is the procession of the sign of the Son of God—the life-giving Cross leads the parade, and when we venerate it joyfully, we praise His glory. This is a celebration that leads us to the greater celebration ahead.

The Holy Cross is placed in the middle of the fast—week three of six. It's very beautiful, actually. Think of Paradise, the Garden of Eden. The Tree of Life was placed in the middle of the Garden of Eden, and here we find the Holy Cross—often said to come from the wood of the Tree of Life, for this wooden Cross is indeed the means to eternal life. The Holy Church places it here to remind us of Adam's sin and to remind us that it is only through the Holy Cross that we will find eternal life.

Today we process with our crosses and sing, "O Lord, save Your people and bless Your inheritance, granting to Your people victory over all their enemies; and by the power of Your Cross, preserving Your Kingdom!"

May God bless all of us through His holy and life-giving Cross!

⁓

What kinds of bad habits might we crucify with Christ during Great Lent?

We work on being less emotionally attached to eating and on fixing our bad habits like fighting, complaining, and gossiping.

Seeing the Holy Cross also reminds us that we are not alone in our struggles. Who else has struggled and suffered?

Jesus struggled and suffered for us.

When Jesus suffered on the Cross, He was able to defeat death. How does this help us as we struggle through Great Lent?

The Cross reminds us that it's through struggle and suffering that we will come to eternal life; we remember that there is a good reason for our struggles.

FOR DISCUSSION: The Tree of Life was planted in the center of the Garden of Eden, and the Cross of Life is planted in the center of Great Lent. Let's list some connections between the Fall of Adam and Eve and the experience of Great Lent. Can you see the connection between the Tree of Life and the Holy Cross?

The Fourth Monday of Great Lent

ONE OF OUR CHURCH'S HOLY saints, Constantine, loved the Holy Cross very much. He was born to Caesar Constantius Chlorus and his wife, Helena, who was a Christian of humble birth, in 274 at Nish, in Serbia. When Constantine was still young, his father divorced his mother because he knew he could be more powerful if he had a richer wife.

Constantine loved his mother and was raised with respect for Christians. The Roman Empire was ruled by four Caesars, and while his father did not hurt Christians in his part of the empire, the other Caesars (including the well-known Emperor Diocletian) were merciless in their persecution of Christians.

When Constantine's father died, Constantine became the ruler of his portion of the Roman Empire (Gaul and Britain), and the first thing he did was to grant freedom of religion throughout his lands: Christians could not be persecuted, and everyone had the right to worship as they wished. This enraged the other rulers in the Empire, and they began to plot to overthrow Constantine.

Constantine would have to go to war to defend his rule. He prayed to God to give him a sign that would inspire his army to fight valiantly, and the Lord showed him the sign of the cross in the heavens with the inscription, "In this sign, conquer." Constantine flew battle flags with the sign of the cross and led his armies against the other rulers of the Roman Empire, defeating them again and again until he was the leader of the Roman Empire. He extended his Edict of Milan to cover all of the Roman Empire: freedom of religion would be protected everywhere in the Empire. After three hundred years of persecution, Christians could finally practice their faith without fear. They could build churches and worship openly.

Constantine would no longer worship false gods, and since Rome was a great center of pagan worship, he moved the capital of the Empire to the city of Byzantium, which would be renamed Constantinople. He built up the city as the first great Christian city, filling it with many beautiful churches and with Christian people.

Emperor Constantine never forgot his victories under the sign of the cross of the Lord, and he wanted to find the actual Cross upon which our Lord Jesus Christ was crucified. He showed great honor to his mother by making her the Empress Helena and sent her to Jerusalem with the authority of the Emperor behind her and a lot of money to build churches and to locate holy places and relics, especially the Cross.

Many years before, the pagan Roman emperors had covered over the location of Christ's Crucifixion and His Tomb in order to keep Christians from worshiping there. They built pagan temples over the top and hoped to erase all memory of Jesus Christ.

When Empress Helena arrived in Jerusalem, she met up with the Patriarch Macarius. Searching for the life-creating Cross, she asked Christians and Jews where it could be, but for a long time they simply could not find it. Finally, someone told her to ask an old man named Jude, who said that the Cross had been buried where the temple of Venus stood. They tore down the pagan temple and, after praying, they began to dig into the ground. Soon the Tomb of the Lord was uncovered. Not far from it were three crosses, a board with the inscription ordered by Pilate, and four nails that had pierced the Lord's body.

They were so excited to find this—but there were three crosses, one for Christ and one for each of the thieves who were crucified with Him. How could they know which of these was Christ's Holy Cross? A funeral procession was happening that day, so Patriarch Macarius touched each of the crosses to the dead man's body. When the True Cross of our Lord touched the dead man, he came to life. When they saw this man raised from the dead, everyone was convinced that this was truly the Life-Giving Cross.

Christians came in huge numbers to venerate the Holy Cross and begged Saint Macarius to stand up the Cross so that even those far off might be able to see it. Then the patriarch and other spiritual leaders raised up the Holy Cross, and the people cried out "Lord, have mercy" and did prostrations in front of it. During the discovery of the life-giving Cross, another miracle took place: a terribly sick woman was healed instantly when she passed under the shadow of the Cross. The old man, Jude, and some other Jews there saw that, and they immediately believed in Christ and accepted Holy Baptism. Jude was baptized with the name Cyriacus and eventually was consecrated Bishop of Jerusalem.

The Holy Empress Helena went to all of the holy places throughout Jerusalem and the Holy Land connected with the earthly life of Jesus Christ, and she built more than eighty churches. She built a church at Bethlehem where Christ was born, at the Garden of Gethsemane where Jesus prayed and was arrested, on the Mount of Olives where He ascended to heaven, and at the tomb of the Holy Theotokos. She also built the Church of the Resurrection (or the Church of the Holy Sepulchre), two connected churches enclosing both the Tomb of Christ and the spot where He was crucified.

St. Helena took part of the Life-Creating Cross and the nails with her back to Constantinople. She died in the year 327, and her son Constantine died in 337. Both are remembered as saints of the Church.

✢

Why didn't the other rulers of the Roman Empire like how Constantine was ruling his portion?

Constantine passed a law giving people the freedom to worship as they pleased, including Christians. The other emperors preferred to arrest and kill Christians.

Constantine had a vision from God, telling him how to win his battles. What was that vision?

The Lord showed him a sign of the cross in the heavens with the inscription, "In this sign, conquer." Constantine flew battle flags with the sign of the cross and won his battles through the power of God.

How did they figure out which of the three buried crosses was the One True and Holy Cross?

Patriarch Macarius touched each of the crosses to a dead man's body. When the True Cross of our Lord touched the dead man, he came back to life, showing that this was truly the life-giving Cross.

For Discussion: Did it surprise you to hear that miracles have happened when people just touched the Holy Cross, or even when they passed beneath its shadow? Even today, there are crosses that have a small piece of the True Cross embedded inside, and people find that miracles happen when they are blessed by them. Why do you think people would be blessed by touching the One True and Holy Cross?

The Fourth Tuesday of Great Lent

I N THE SCRIPTURES, JESUS TELLS us that we should pick up our cross. What does that mean?

In Matthew 16, Jesus is telling the disciples that He will be killed and then raised on the third day, and then He says:

> If anyone desires to come after Me, let him deny himself, and take up his cross, and follow Me. For whoever desires to save his life will lose it, but whoever loses his life for My sake will find it. For what profit is it to a man if he gains the whole world, and loses his own soul? Or what will a man give in exchange for his soul? For the Son of Man will come in the glory of His Father with His angels, and then He will reward each according to his works. Assuredly, I say to you, there are some standing here who shall not taste death till they see the Son of Man coming in His kingdom. (Matt. 16:24–27)

Jesus has just described His own death, and then He tells His disciples to deny themselves and pick up their own crosses and follow Him. What does that mean?

The disciples followed Christ very literally: they walked with Him everywhere He went, learning from Him and working with Him to preach, teach, and heal people. After His Resurrection and Ascension to heaven, the Holy Spirit came to them at Pentecost, and they went out into the world to preach His gospel. They left their families and their lives behind. Christ sets up two paths for us: we can try to gain the world, or we can try to save our souls. If we hope to gain the world by seeking after worldly prizes like money or fame, then we will lose our souls. The disciples dropped everything when Christ called them to join Him, and they were willing to lose their lives. In fact, all of the disciples except for John would eventually be martyred for preaching the Resurrection of Jesus Christ.

What does picking up our cross and following Christ look like in our lives? It will mean different things for each of us. Everyone has different challenges in their lives. A person with a really bad temper may find that struggling with angry outbursts is their cross to bear, while a person who has no patience will find that this is their cross. Some people might have health challenges, while others have trouble making friends or struggle with school. Some people look as if they have no struggles, but there will always be some kind of challenge for them, whether we can see it or not. We can choose to complain and pout about our struggles, or we can take a deep breath and pick up our cross as Jesus did: He did not deserve the Cross, but He carried it and faced it with patience, forgiveness, and peace. We should all hope to follow His example and to face our obstacles prayerfully.

Following Christ may look different for different people, but it always begins with working to soften our hearts so that when Christ calls us to something, we are ready to answer "Yes." The main thing we must do is to put aside worries about our comfort and our desires and instead focus on loving God with all our hearts and loving our neighbors as ourselves. If we can choose to serve others instead of making ourselves more comfortable or making our lives easier, then we are getting closer and closer to being able to live a good Christian life. When we follow Christ's commandments, we are developing soft hearts that can be filled with God's grace.

ॐ

How did Jesus' disciples pick up their crosses and follow Him?

They walked around the world preaching the gospel and were per-secuted and martyred when they would not stop.

What do we mean when we say that different people have different crosses to bear?

Different people have different challenges in their lives (maybe they have a temper or a medical condition, etc.).

How did Jesus carry His Cross?

Even though Jesus did not deserve the Cross, He carried it and faced it with patience, forgiveness, and peace.

FOR DISCUSSION: What are the crosses in your life today? Do you think they will change over time, or will you always struggle with the same ones?

The Fourth Wednesday of Great Lent

IN THE SCRIPTURES WE FIND the story of Naaman the Leper, who carried the cross of leprosy and found healing through humility. (If you'd like to find this story in your Bible, it's in 4 Kingdoms/2 Kings, chapter 5.)

Naaman, the commander of the army of Syria, was a great and honorable man in the eyes of his master because he achieved great military victories. He was a great warrior, but he also suffered from leprosy, which is a disease that makes body parts rot and fall off. It was a terrible illness. Naaman's wife had a young servant who happened to be from Israel, and one day she said to the wife, "If only my master were with the prophet of God Elisha! He would cure my master's leprosy!" And Naaman's wife went in and told her husband, saying, "This is what the girl from the land of Israel said."

Then the king of Syria said to Naaman, "Go now, and I will send a letter to the king of Israel." So he departed and took with him ten talents of silver, six thousand gold shekels, and ten changes of clothing. Naaman was introduced with this letter, which proved that he was a very important visitor. Hearing that Naaman had come to see him, the Prophet Elisha told the king of Israel, "Let Naaman come to me, and he shall know there is a prophet in Israel."

Then Naaman went with his horses and chariot and stood at

the door of Elisha's house. And Elisha sent a messenger out to him, saying, "Go and bathe in the Jordan River seven times, and your flesh shall be restored to you, and you shall be clean."

But Naaman became furious and went away, saying, "Indeed, I told myself that Elisha would come out to greet me; that he would stand and call on the name of his God; and that he would put his hand upon the place and heal the leprosy. Are not the rivers of Damascus better than all the waters of Israel? Can I not bathe in them and be clean?" So he turned and went away very angry.

Then his servants approached and said to him, "If the prophet were to tell you to do something great and difficult, wouldn't you do it? But instead the prophet said to you, 'Bathe and be clean.'"

So Naaman went down and dipped seven times in the Jordan River, according to Elisha's instruction, and his flesh was restored like the flesh of a little child, and he was cleansed. His leprosy was healed.

Then he, with all his aides, returned to Elisha and came and stood before him; and he said, "Indeed, now I have come to know that in all the earth there is no God except the God of Israel."

The Prophet Elisha said to Naaman, "Go in peace."

Even before the accomplished and powerful leader Naaman came before him, the Prophet Elisha seemed to know what he needed to learn in order to be healed: the man of God told the king of Israel, "Let Naaman come to me, and he shall know there is a prophet in Israel." Naaman needed to be healed of both his leprosy and his pride, and he needed to get to know God.

When Naaman arrived at the prophet's home, he stood outside the gate and assumed that the prophet would invite him in. He expected to be honored as an important guest, but instead a mere servant simply gave him some simple instructions. The prophet did not greet him in person and did not make a big deal of him, but instead simply sent a servant with advice for healing.

At first, Naaman reacted pridefully. He was insulted that the prophet did not personally welcome him and meet with him or touch him to heal him. The prophet didn't do the things that Naaman expected. So, he turned away in anger. He even tried to insult Israel as he had been insulted, saying that the rivers of his homeland were better than Israel's rivers. Naaman expected to be treated well because he was such an important man, which is prideful. What's more, he had an image of what that healing would look like: "Indeed, I told myself that Elisha would come out to greet me; that he would stand and call on the name of his God; and that he would put his hand upon the place and heal the leprosy." He was furious when the healing of God did not look as he expected it to look.

We are all guilty of this kind of pride sometimes. We may not be important military leaders, but we are people who think we know what healing looks like, and we get impatient and even angry with God when His answers to our prayers are not what we expect. If I pray that God heals my brother's wounds, I expect Him to heal them on my schedule and in the way I have imagined. When God heals in His own way and on His own timetable, it sometimes helps us to remember that we are not in charge, but truly God is. We must work to accept His will rather than demand that He do things our way.

Naaman almost walked away from healing, but he was lucky, and his wise servants pointed out his error. They said, "If the prophet were to tell you to do something great and difficult, wouldn't you do it? But instead the prophet said to you, 'Bathe and be clean.'" In other words, if the prophet had given him a task that sounded hard or important, he would have done it, but because the task was so small and simple, he was offended. His servants suggested that he set his pride and his expectations aside and try bathing in the Jordan River. Luckily for Naaman, his servants were wise and were not blinded by pride as he was.

This is the turning point: Naaman stopped being prideful and took advice from his own servants. He humbled himself and listened. He had been offended when the servants of the prophet had offered him this message, but now he corrected that and took his servants' advice to listen to Elisha's servants. He went to the Jordan River and bathed in it seven times, and he was healed forever of his terrible leprosy.

When Naaman was able to overcome his pride and to approach with humility, his leprosy was healed and his eyes were opened. He said, "Indeed, now I have come to know that in all the earth there is no God except the God of Israel." He was given both good health and strong faith in God.

In Naaman's case, the cross he carried was his leprosy. He struggled with this terrible health condition for years. Perhaps his pride was also a cross, though he did not know it. When he brought his cross to the man of God to ask for help, he was given relief from both crosses.

We may not realize it, but when we pray the prayers for healing in the Church, we most often pray words like, "Lord, please grant healing of soul and body." We may be most focused on our bodily illnesses, and we are probably praying for people because we have seen that they are physically sick or suffering, but God heals both the soul and the body. God knows that our eternal lives depend on the health of our souls, which is much more important than our physical health. Sometimes we expect healing to look a certain way, but in fact what God sends is different from our expectations and much better for us. Like Naaman, when we come to the Lord for healing, if we can humble ourselves we will find that God sends both spiritual and physical healing.

꒰

Naaman was an important man. What did he expect to happen when he came to the prophet's home?

Naaman expected to be welcomed in like an important guest and for the prophet to touch him to heal the leprosy.

What was Naaman's cross?

Naaman's cross to bear was leprosy, and also his pride was a cross (though he may not have known it).

What was the turning point that allowed Naaman to be healed?

When Naaman set aside his pride and listened to his own wise servants and the advice from the Prophet Elisha's servants, he could be healed.

FOR DISCUSSION: Can you think of a time when you prayed for help from God with a certain expectation, but the help looked different than you expected? Were you confused and angry like Naaman? Why or why not?

The Fourth Thursday of Great Lent

A S WE CONSIDER THE CROSS of Jesus Christ this week, we find the related themes of humility and self-sacrifice. The modern saint Mother Maria of Paris is a wonderful example of self-sacrifice.

When she was born in 1891, her parents named her Elizaveta Pilenko, but everyone called her Liza. Liza grew up in Latvia, which was part of the Russian Empire, and her father was the mayor of her town. Both of her parents were devout Orthodox Christians. As a little girl, she once emptied her piggy bank in order to give all of her money to a fund to paint an icon for a new church in her town. When she was seven, she asked her mom if she could become a nun, and then a year later she asked her parents if she could become a pilgrim who just walks from holy place to holy place forever. As a child, she loved God very much and hoped to devote her life to Him.

When she was fourteen, her beloved father died, and Liza went through a very difficult time. She grew angry with God and became an atheist. She felt that her father's death was meaningless and unjust. "If there is no justice," she said, "there is no God." She decided that all of the adults knew there was no God, and they were just pretending for the children.

After her father's death, the family moved to the big city of St. Petersburg, where Liza became friends with a group of revolutionaries—that is, a group of people who wanted to make big changes in their country. Liza wanted to be a part of something very big that would fix her country's problems and make it a better place. She yearned to sacrifice, to lay her life on the line to fight for justice. She was disappointed, though, because all the revolutionaries seemed to do was talk. They had a lot of ideas, but they never did anything big. She said, "My spirit longed to engage in heroic feats, even to perish, to combat the injustice of the world." She wanted to do something heroic, but all they ever did was sit and talk.

At age nineteen, she married one of the these revolutionaries from the group, and they all sat together in cafés, discussing politics and poetry and theology. Though Liza still thought of herself as an atheist, she became interested in Jesus Christ, at first not as her God, but simply as a heroic man who accomplished great things. Over time, she found herself drawn back toward the Church, and she began to believe in God again. She prayed and read the Gospels and the lives of saints. She decided that what the people really needed was not a revolution but Jesus Christ.

Liza and her husband had a daughter named Gaiana, but their marriage ended in divorce. Liza became the first female student at the Theological Academy of the Alexander Nevsky Monastery in St. Petersburg, and for a while in 1918, Liza was the mayor of her town, as her father had been. Unfortunately, this was during the time that the Bolsheviks were taking over Russia, and she was accused of helping them and then arrested and taken to trial. Her judge, Daniel Skobstova, said she was innocent, and after she was free, she went to find him to thank him. They quickly became friends and were married only a few days later.

Right after the wedding, as the Bolsheviks got stronger in Russia, Liza and her whole family left the country. They didn't want to be part of all the horrible things that happen during a revolution. They traveled quite a bit and then settled in Paris, France. The couple had two more children. In the winter of 1926, Liza's whole family got influenza. Their youngest daughter, little Anastasia, died from it. But this time, a death in her family did not drive Liza away from the Faith: instead, her faith grew stronger. She wanted to live a more real, more pure Christian life than ever, and she began to dedicate all of her time and energy to working to help Russian refugees in Paris. Sadly, all of this work was hard on her marriage to Daniel, and she left him, moved into her mother's house, and continued her work.

In 1932, Metropolitan Evlogy tonsured her a nun and encouraged her to develop a new kind of monasticism: the life of a nun living in the city and serving the needy people there instead of living out alone in the countryside. So Liza, now Mother Maria, began her work of sharing her life with the poor and homeless.

She started with just one small, empty house, and she filled it with Russian refugees who needed help. Over time she added more and more houses. She cooked for everyone and took care of them, serving up to 120 every night. Each house had a chapel, and Mother Maria would even make the icons for the chapel herself. Often Orthodox speakers would come and speak during dinner, inspiring the refugees living there. Mother Maria started a hospital and some schools for children. She was doing so much! She helped start an organization called Orthodox Action, which put faith into action—helping the poor, the old, the sick, and the unemployed. Mother Maria was living up to her youthful dream of really doing something for change, not just talking about it.

When the Holocaust began and edged closer to Paris, of course Mother Maria did all she could to help save the Jewish people who reached out for help. Her priest, Fr. Dimitri Klepinin, made baptismal certificates for any Jewish person who asked for one, even if they were not really converting, because any Jew that had a certificate saying they had converted to Christianity was in less danger. Mother Maria, her son Yura, and Fr. Dimitri then planned escape routes for the Jewish people who asked them for help.

In 1942, the Nazis were holding many of the Jews in a huge stadium, called the Velodrome d'Hiver. They would hold people in the stadium for a few days and then send them, packed onto trains, to death camps. Mother Maria somehow entered the stadium and spent time trying to find ways to help the people held there. Amazingly, she made some arrangements with the trash haulers who were taking garbage out of the stadium, and they helped her sneak Jewish children out of the Velodrome to safety. They put the children inside trash cans, then drove them in garbage trucks to Mother Maria's house, where she would help to arrange for their escape from Paris. It was very dangerous, but Mother Maria was grateful to be able to save precious lives.

The Nazis finally caught Mother Maria in 1943. They arrested her for helping the Jewish people and took her to Ravensbruck, one of the concentration camps. Even while she was a prisoner in that Nazi camp, Mother Maria was helping people. One survivor talked about her later and said everyone adored her, especially the young prisoners. They had been separated from their families, but Mother Maria became their family and cared for them. She was known to give her meal (a piece of bread) to anyone that she thought needed it more than she did. She lived this way until she died.

On Great and Holy Friday that year, April 30, 1945, Mother Maria was killed in a gas chamber. We are not sure if she was selected to die that day or if she volunteered to take someone else's place. Either way, she died because of the way she lived her faith.

Mother Maria was truly a woman of action. She once said, "At the Last Judgment I shall not be asked whether I was successful in my ascetic exercises, nor how many bows and prostrations I made. Instead I shall be asked, did I feed the hungry, clothe the naked, visit the sick and the prisoners. That is all I shall be asked." And she lived exactly that way. But she went beyond just feeding, clothing, visiting, and helping the others in her care: she actually saw everyone she met as "the very icon of God incarnate in the world," and she treated them as such. She may even have died in the place of one of those icons of God, walking out the Faith to the very last moment of her earthly life.

☙

What sorts of ideas did little Liza have for her life when she was young?

She talked about being a nun or traveling as a pilgrim from holy place to holy place.

How did Mother Maria and Fr. Dimitri help Jewish people, and what did the Nazis do when they found out?

Mother Maria smuggled children in trash cans out of the stadium to save them, and Fr. Dimitri gave out false baptismal certificates to anyone who asked. Together, they worked to hide Jewish people in her house and to smuggle them away. When the Nazis learned of their activities, they were placed in concentration camps.

What was Mother Maria's idea of what it meant to follow Christ?

She took very seriously Jesus' words that we are feeding and serving Him when we feed and serve the least of these, so she dedicated herself to taking care of people in need.

FOR DISCUSSION: There are many different saints, and each one is unique. Mother Maria was different from most other saints. She had a rougher way of carrying herself, she was divorced twice, and she was outspoken. She picked up her cross and followed Christ in her own way, using the gifts God gave her and the circumstances He put her in. God is glorious in His saints. What are your gifts? If you dedicate your life to serving Christ, how will it look different from someone else's life?

The Fourth Friday of Great Lent

WHEN WE THINK OF A life marked by humility and loving self-sacrifice, we might think of St. Xenia of St. Petersburg. We don't know much about St. Xenia's childhood, but we do know that she was married to Major Andrei Feodorovich Petrov, who died very suddenly one night at a party. At the age of twenty-six, Xenia was a widow, and it seemed to everyone that she lost her mind from grief: she told everyone that she had died and that Andrei had lived. She gave away all of her possessions to the poor, dressed herself in her dead husband's military uniform, and, as if she had completely forgotten her own name and identity, she began to call herself by her husband's name, Andrei Feodorovich.

But Xenia had not lost her mind at all. She had become a fool for Christ. Sometimes very holy people pretend to have lost their minds. This allows them a certain freedom, because when they behave in a way that makes people think that they are out of their minds, they can stop worrying about people's opinions of them. Rather than try to convince people that they are good or holy or smart, they allow people to think they're crazy and instead focus on their relationship with God. So often, a love of stuff and money and a desire to be admired by others can become the center of our hearts. The fool for Christ throws off all of these things and hopes to fill her heart only with God.

Xenia had lost her husband, and that grief brought her closer to God. She gave her house to a friend, asking that she allow homeless and poor people to shelter there. Instead of living there too, Xenia wandered among the poor people, and at night she went out into a field to pray in the silence.

Xenia was very concerned that her beloved husband had died so suddenly and at a party. She knew that it would be better if he had had time to go to confession and to receive Holy Communion before he died. She worried that he was not properly prepared for heaven. She prayed for him, and she decided to do good works in his name so that God would give all of the credit for those works to Andrei. She knew that our Lord teaches us to look not for rewards on earth but to build up our treasure in heaven, and she set about building her beloved Andrei some treasure in heaven.

A construction crew started to build a church in the Smolensk Cemetery. Xenia saw an opportunity for a good deed, and every night she would secretly come to the worksite and carry bricks up to the top of the construction. She was helping the bricklayers build the church, though they didn't know who was doing it. Xenia did it in the name of her husband, hoping that God would receive it on his behalf and let it become his treasure in heaven.

The people of St. Petersburg began to see that this woman who walked among them was holy. They could sense the light of Christ inside her. Whenever Xenia entered anyone's home, they said it was a good sign. Mothers were delighted if she kissed their children. Cab drivers asked permission of the blessed one to drive her a little, since after this their earnings would be guaranteed for the whole day. Storekeepers tried to give her a little bit of bread because they wanted their store to be blessed by her—they were sure to do good business if Xenia came by.

Xenia did not want to be well known for her holiness, and yet she really could not hide it.

God even gave Xenia the gift of clairvoyance, which means that sometimes she could predict the future. On the eve of the Nativity of Jesus Christ in 1762, she kept telling everyone in St. Petersburg, "Tomorrow all Russia will bake blini!" Blini are a kind of pancake they would make for funerals, and quite suddenly the next morning, the Empress Elizabeth Petrovna died. Indeed, all of Russia did bake blini.

Once, Xenia was visiting a home where the daughter was grown up but still unmarried. She said to the girl, "Here you are drinking coffee while your husband is burying his wife at Okhta." The girl did not know it yet, but eventually she would marry a man who, at that very moment, was burying his first wife at the Okhta Cemetery.

Saint Xenia lived about forty-five years as a fool for Christ, living without the comforts of home and dedicating herself to doing good works in the name of her husband. She wanted no credit for anything she had done. She was buried in the Smolensk Cemetery, where she had helped build the church.

People make pilgrimages to her grave and ask for her intercession when they are facing troubles. Saint Xenia has appeared in visions to people, warning them of dangers to come and saving them from terrible situations.

Pray for us, St. Xenia!

※

When St. Xenia's husband died, what strange things did she do?

She began calling herself by his name, dressing in his clothes, and giving away all of her possessions.

Why do fools for Christ want people to think they have lost their minds?

When people assume that they have lost their minds, they can just go off and live on the streets without worrying about their possessions or what people think of them.

If being humble means that we do not brag or show off, could we say that St. Xenia was humble?

By living among the poor and hoping that all of her good deeds would be credited to her husband, Andrei, Saint Xenia showed that she was extremely humble. She did not want credit or fame for anything she did.

FOR DISCUSSION: This week is the week of the Cross, and when we think of Saint Xenia, can we say that she sacrificed herself for others? How?

The Fourth Saturday of Great Lent

A S WE FINISH THE WEEK dedicated to the Cross of Jesus Christ, we close with the stories of two very modern saints, both of whom impressed the world with their humility and self-sacrifice.

In Bulgaria, there lived a man named Dobri Dimitrov Dobrev (often called Grandpa Dobri, or Elder Dobri), who appeared to be a beggar on the streets. He was born on July 20, 1914, in the village of Bailovo. His father died in World War I, and his mother raised the children. In 1940, he got married while his nation, Bulgaria, was participating in the Second World War. A shell fell near him during one of the bombings in Sofia and ruined his hearing. He and his wife had four children.

Over the years, Dobri became less and less concerned with money and stuff and slowly started devoting himself entirely to the spiritual life. Around the year 2000, he donated all of his belongings to the Orthodox Church and began living in a small building in the yard of the Ss. Cyril and Methodius Church in his native village. Although there was a bed in his tiny house, he preferred to sleep on the floor, and he kept just enough food for a day or two—perhaps just one slice of bread and a tomato.

The old church needed many repairs, and so old Dobri—even in his nineties—could be seen on a wintry morning, rolling up the sleeves of his old black coat and carrying full buckets and boards around the church yard, helping with the work of roof repairs and the like. Despite his old age, he was happy to assist the workers as best he could.

Not only did Elder Dobri help out with the work—it turns out that he was helping to pay for it. You see, around the same time that he began to live in the church yard, he also started to collect money toward the restoration of that church and the other churches and monasteries throughout Bulgaria. He would walk more than twelve and a half miles to reach the capital city of Sofia from his village. He did this for many years, until his legs began to lose strength, so he started taking the bus. He stood at the entrance to the Alexander Nevsky Cathedral in Sofia with a plastic cup in his hand and collected money from the people who passed by, then donated that money to rebuild churches.

Elder Dobri was not afraid of cold weather and did not fear hunger. He didn't mind it when people walked past him without giving something. Instead, he simply radiated kindness and meekness and love. He might reach out and kiss a child's hand with a smile or spend a few moments speaking with someone about the mercy of God. When people put some money into his cup, he would give them a loving look and thank them for their charity. His loving smiles and constant presence made him a great favorite of the people of Bulgaria, and soon they were calling him the saint of Bailovo.

Over the years, he collected about $24,700 for the cathedral in Sofia, $12,350 for the Ss. Cyril and Methodius Church in Bailovo, and $31,000 for the restoration of the Eleshnishki Monastery of the Mother of God, located to the east of Sofia, and the local church of the Gorno Kamartsi village.

Elder Dobri fell asleep in the Lord at the age of 103 on February 13, 2018, and was buried in the graveyard of the Ss. Cyril and Methodius Church in the town where he was born—Bailovo, Bulgaria. May his memory be eternal! Those who remember his holiness already call out, "Pray for us, Elder Dobri!"

Perhaps one day the Church will recognize Elder Dobri as a saint—but already, so many Bulgarians and people around the world remember the lessons they learned from watching his good example.

Not every holy and humble person is a fool for Christ. It is possible to hold a well-respected office in the world or in the Church while also living a humble, self-sacrificing, holy life.

A recent patriarch of the Serbian Orthodox Church was well known for his holiness. He was born Gojko Stojcevic on September 11, 1914 (the same year as dear Elder Dobri). His family did not have much money, and unfortunately both of his parents died when he was very young. He was raised by his aunt and once said, "When you grow up without parents, you experience a greater awareness of the heavenly Father."

Gojko became a monk, then a priest, and was given the new name Pavle (which is Serbian for Paul, like St. Paul). He never wanted to be patriarch, but he was so well loved and such a holy man that he was chosen for this important role.

Patriarch Pavle was famous for refusing to ride in a fancy car with a driver. He either walked or rode on public transportation in the city; he went through the crowds without guards or assistants. Anyone could walk right up to him and have a chat. He was very available to the people, all of the time.

He was known for his modest lifestyle. It is said that one day, as he was walking to the offices of the patriarchate, Patriarch Pavle noticed some expensive cars parked near the entrance and asked whose cars they were. His assistant told him that they belonged to the bishops. At that, the patriarch said with a smile, "If they who know the Savior's commandment on poverty have such cars, then what kind of car would they have if there wasn't this commandment?"

Patriarch Pavle was especially beloved for his shoes. You see, he always wore old scruffy shoes. Often people would come to visit him and to receive a blessing or discuss some important business, and they would realize that his shoes were old and had holes in them. Often they would buy him a new pair of shoes, nice ones befitting a man as important as the patriarch. He was famous for putting on beautiful shoes and heading out into the street, where he would promptly trade shoes with a poor man sitting on a stoop. The nice shoes went out to the needy, and the patriarch wore whatever was left. One time a woman was meeting with him, and just as she was about to suggest that he needed new shoes, the patriarch burst out with great glee, "See what great shoes I have! I found them near the dustbins when I went to the patriarchate. Somebody threw 'em out, but they're real leather. I sewed 'em a bit. . . . See, they'll last for a long time yet."

He could not only repair shoes or cobble himself new boots from old women's shoes, but if he saw a priest with a torn cassock or cloak, he said to him, "Bring it to me; I'll fix it." Even though he was the patriarch and an old man, he did the preparations before the services himself, and he cleaned up afterward, washed the utensils, and hung up his own cassock and cowl. He heard the confessions of the faithful and gave them Communion. Like many great ascetics, he didn't eat much. He lived a humble and modest life and was beloved by his people.

He fell asleep in the Lord in 2009, and many people pray to ask for his intercessions. Perhaps someday he will be a saint of the Church.

The Church offers us many examples of people whose lives are centered on God instead of centered on themselves and their own needs. This looks different for everyone, but ultimately we are all called to find a way to pick up our cross and to follow Christ. We use the gifts He has given us, and we find a way to serve Him—whether we serve Him by serving the Church, serving the poor, or serving the ordinary people He places in our path every day. Especially during this beautiful season of Great Lent, let's watch for opportunities to serve God and others.

ॐ

People thought Elder Dobri was an ordinary beggar on the street until one day they realized that he did something special with the money he collected. What did he do with it?

He funded the restoration of churches and monasteries across Bulgaria.

Where did he move?

To a small building outside the church in his village, where he slept on the floor and lived as simply as he could.

Patriarch Pavle was famous for his shoes. Why?

He refused to wear nice shoes but would always wear old, shabby shoes that he had fixed up or shoes he'd traded with a poor or homeless person.

FOR DISCUSSION: These examples of saintly people are from modern times. Do you know anyone who lives a saintly life? We are all called to become saints, but that call looks different for every one of us. Discuss ways that you might live out that calling in your own life, in your own circumstances.

The Sunday of St. John Climacus

TODAY IS THE SUNDAY OF St. John Climacus, and we should begin by saying that *Climacus* is not his name—it's a word that means "ladder." Saint John wrote a book called *The Ladder of Divine Ascent,* so we call him St. John Climacus, or St. John of the Ladder.

Saint John was very smart and well educated. He could have become a famous teacher, but he decided instead that he wanted to serve God with his whole heart by becoming a monk. At just sixteen years old, he joined a monastery in a very special place called Mt. Sinai, which is where Moses once climbed to the top of the mountain and received the Ten Commandments from God.

Saint John lived at the monastery for many years, then decided to go live alone in the desert, like a hermit. For forty years, he spent all of his time praying and reading the lives of the saints.

At first, St. John was tempted by the devil, and he felt all kinds of bad passions trying to make him sin. But he put all his trust in Jesus and prayed harder than ever. The more he was tempted, the more he prayed—so the temptations never made him fall into sin. In fact, he only grew holier. He became so close to God that many of the other monks and the people heard how holy he was, and they came to ask him for advice.

Saint John spent so much time overcoming temptation in the desert that God gave him a special gift: he could help upset and tempted people find peace. One time, a man who was having terrible temptations asked St. John to help him, and after they prayed together, the poor man's soul was filled with peace instead of struggle and difficulty. He was never again troubled with those temptations.

Saint John took on a disciple named Moses. One afternoon, Moses walked a long way away to find some dirt for their little garden (remember, they lived in the desert). He lay down to take a rest under a large rock. Saint John was back home in his cell, but God showed him that Moses was in danger, and he started praying. That evening, when Moses returned, he told St. John that during his nap he was almost crushed by a huge rock. But in his sleep he heard the voice of St. John calling to him, and he hopped up—just as the rock began to break away and fall.

When St. John was seventy-four years old, he was chosen as abbot of Mt. Sinai. He became the superior of all the monks and hermits in the area, and they asked him to write down the rules he had followed throughout his life. He was very holy, and the other monks wanted to follow his example. So St. John wrote the book called *The Ladder of Perfection* or *The Ladder of Divine Ascent*.

Saint John was a leader among the monastics on Mt. Sinai. Just as Moses had once climbed this mountain and come down with a list of Ten Commandments from God for the people to follow, St. John was climbing a spiritual mountain and returning with a collection of rules for the monastic to follow. He was like a new Moses, who had come down from Mt. Sinai with his face aglow from meeting God, delivering *The Ladder* with its thirty steps, which over the centuries is still beloved and is considered the ultimate guide to living a Christian ascetic life.

✌

Saint John went through many temptations. Did they cause him to sin? Why not?

Saint John responded to temptations by praying even more, so the temptations never overcame him.

Why is he called St. John Climacus?

Climacus means "of the ladder"; he is known by this name because he wrote The Ladder of Divine Ascent.

What do the prophet Moses and St. John have in common?

There are a few things that connect them, including the fact that they both were at Mt. Sinai and received instructions from God to pass along to the people. (Moses offered the Ten Commandments, and St. John offered The Ladder.*)*

FOR DISCUSSION: If you had to guess what steps St. John would put in his ladder to becoming closer to God, what would they be?

The Fifth Monday of Great Lent

THIS WEEK WE ARE THINKING about St. John's *Ladder of Divine Ascent*. After spending years fighting the passions and temptation, St. John wrote *The Ladder* to show us how to follow him on this path toward Christ. He included thirty steps we could take to make this journey.

St. John's *Ladder* is written for monastics, so the steps begin with leaving the world behind. Then slowly he reveals the different passions and temptations his readers will have to battle—and he explains how to win those battles.

The Ladder is also loved by Orthodox Christians who are not in monasteries. The same temptations and challenges face all Christians as they try to live a good, Orthodox life.

For example, the first step is renouncing the world—this means giving up the world, or choosing to leave the world behind. This is not just a question that monks must face. Every Christian must begin by choosing a Christian life instead of a worldly life, choosing heavenly rewards over earthly pleasures. For a monastic, this means that they will leave the city behind, leave their friends and family and worldly possessions, and go live in a religious community where their life will focus on prayer and spiritual development. But what would it mean for someone who lives in the world, who stays in the city and works at a regular job or raises a regular family? How does that ordinary person choose a Christian life and renounce the world?

In his letter to the Romans, St. Paul writes, "Do not conform to the pattern of this world, but be transformed by the renewing of your mind" (Rom. 12:2 NIV). All of us, no matter what our circumstances, can do this. We can choose not to fit ourselves to the pattern of this world. We can choose not to do something just because it's normal or because that's what everyone does. We can decide that instead of doing what everyone else is doing, we are going to always focus on what God wants us to do.

Saint Paisios said, "Do not trust the mindset of secular people. . . . Decide what you want most: the sympathy of the world, or a return near to God?" This does not mean that we do not love people who are not in the Church—we hope to love everyone as we love ourselves. But it does mean that we have to recognize that some people are not working to be closer to God. So if we do wish to grow close to God, then we will make our decisions differently than they do, because we are working on a different project than they are.

For example, the people around us may not even know that it's Great Lent, but we can follow Christ and follow the Church by making sure that we mark these days with prayer and fasting and almsgiving. We can work to make sure that our hearts are being formed to the pattern God created for us. We'll be transformed by Christ as we work to tame the passions and temptations we encounter along the way. In this way, we are still living in the world among all of the different kinds of people here, but we are living in a way that is dedicated to God.

A wonderful saint who lived in the twentieth century, St. Porphyrios, was once assigned as a priest to a church in a very busy part of Athens called Omonia Square. It was kind of a dirty neighborhood with a lot of poor people and a lot of crime. And it was so loud there in the middle of the city. While he would try to celebrate the holy services of the Church, the noise from the street was terribly loud. He even had one neighbor who sold gramophones and records. The shopkeeper played records on the gramophone in order to attract customers, but he played them so loudly that St. Porphyrios could not bear it. At first he was frustrated by this, and he was tempted to ask to be sent to a different parish. But holy St. Porphyrios prayed and fasted for three days, asking God to help him.

In the corner of his church, St. Porphyrios found a notebook that belonged to a young man in his parish, a student at the university. It was a physics notebook, and in it the saint found some notes about acoustic waves and how sound travels. Saint Porphyrios thought about how, if you throw a pebble into a lake, it creates circles that move outward. But if you throw another rock into another section of the lake, it creates new, even bigger circles, and they push out the other circles.

This was the answer from God that St. Porphyrios was waiting for. The next day, he tried to concentrate all his spiritual and mental powers into the prayers and the acts of the Divine Liturgy. He saw himself forming circles in his mind and heart, and they canceled out the wave circles formed by the gramophone. The sounds stopped distracting him from the Divine Liturgy, and he was able to focus again.

If we are finding it hard to focus on God when we are living in this world full of distractions, we must pray about it and keep trying. It is possible to live a holy life even in the middle of so much noise, and God will help us find a way.

In the book *Wounded by Love*, St. Porphyrios wrote:

> It is a great art to succeed in having your soul sanctified. A person can become a saint anywhere. He can become a saint in Omonia Square, if he wants. At your

work, whatever it may be, you can become a saint through meekness, patience, and love. Make a new start every day, with new resolution, with enthusiasm and love, prayer and silence—not with anxiety so that you get a pain in the chest.

We must not worry and be anxious about whether the world around us is dedicated to God. We must simply decide to behave like true Christians and follow Christ with love and prayer, and we can become saints anywhere. We will simply carve out our little piece of the Kingdom in this world, patterning it not after the world's ideas but after Christ's example.

ॐ

The Ladder is written for monastics and begins with the first step of renouncing the world. If we don't leave the world for a monastery, can we as Christians still renounce the world?

Yes, all Christians make the choice to follow Christ instead of following everyone else.

If we are Christians, will we make decisions differently than our non-Christian friends?

Yes, because we are working to grow closer to God, but they are not on that same journey.

Saint Porphyrios found that he could serve the liturgy even with so much noise surrounding his church. What helped him do that?

He envisioned the sound-wave ripples of the other sounds, and the ripples of the prayers he was sending out, and he saw that his prayer ripples were pushing out the other sounds.

FOR DISCUSSION: In what ways are you surrounded by noise and distraction? How are you focusing on your Lenten journey and your Christian journey in the midst of these other worldly things?

The Fifth Tuesday of Great Lent

I N St. John Climacus's *Ladder of Divine Ascent*, there are many steps, but today we will consider just two: steps 16 and 17, which are related to the important Lenten theme of almsgiving.

Let's consider what Jesus teaches us about riches. In Luke 18:18–27, we read:

> A certain ruler asked Him, "Good Teacher, what must I do to inherit eternal life?"
>
> "Why do you call Me good?" Jesus answered. "No one is good—except God alone. You know the commandments: 'You shall not commit adultery, you shall not murder, you shall not steal, you shall not give false tesitmony, honor your father and mother.'"
>
> "All these things I have kept since I was a boy," he said.
>
> When Jesus heard this, he said to him, "You still lack one thing. Sell everything you have and give to the poor, and you will have treasure in heaven. Then come, follow Me."
>
> When he heard this, he became very sad, because he was very wealthy.
>
> Jesus looked at him and said, "How hard it is for the rich to enter the kingdom of God! Indeed, it is easier for a camel to go through the eye of a needle than for someone who is rich to enter the kingdom of God."
>
> Those who heard this asked, "Who then can be saved?"
>
> Jesus replied, "What is impossible with man is possible with God."

This young man wants to know what else he can do to become more holy, but he does not like Jesus' answer: he does not like the idea of giving away all of his riches. He becomes sorrowful, which means "full of sadness and pain." Jesus says that it is hard for the rich to enter the kingdom of God because they are so attached to their riches. They love their riches more than they love the Kingdom.

We saw at the beginning of *The Ladder* that the Christian life begins with choosing to pick up our cross and follow Christ, to lead a God-centered life, and to renounce the world. In rules 16 and 17, we will see that we can work our way up the ladder by renouncing money and possessions as well. Saint John explains that we will have to choose between loving money and loving God. We cannot do both. He urges us to become non-possessive; that means that we must stop feeling like we want to own things and keep them for ourselves. We need to be able to love something without wanting to own it.

Saint John says that "a non-possessive monk is lord of the world. He has entrusted his cares to God, and by faith he has obtained all men as his servants. He will not tell his need to man, and he receives what comes to him as from the hand of the Lord." When we have become non-possessive (meaning that we have stopped caring so much about owning things), we trust completely that God will send whatever we need, as we need it. Instead of trying to own everything we will ever need and holding it tight, we turn to God. We trust that if we need something, He will send it. We pray to God for our needs, but we don't mention them to anyone else because of our complete faith that God will send what we need. And then when someone gives us what we need, we thank God and recognize that it was really God who sent it.

There is a great Church Father named St. Basil the Great who truly worked to keep himself from becoming greedy and loving to own things. He was very well educated and wealthy, but he sold off his inheritance and gave all of the money he received to the poor.

Saint Basil loved monasticism, but he did not love the idea of living far away from the city full of people that God loves so much. He loved to pray for the poor and the sick, but he wanted even more to really serve them. He took Christ's commandment to love your neighbor as yourself very seriously and preached about the problem of the rich who allow their neighbors to suffer. He often spoke about that rich young man who was so filled with sorrow when Jesus told him to give away all of his possessions.

In the early Church, they talked about that young man a lot. The famous St. Clement of Alexandria saw that the young man loved his stuff so much, he could not be free; he was held tight by his love for stuff. Saint Clement said that the young man did not really have to give away all of his stuff, but Jesus wanted him to stop loving it so much.

But St. Basil would emphasize something else in this passage. You see, Jesus did not just say, "If you wish to be perfect, go sell your possessions." He actually said, "Go sell your possessions and give to the poor." St. Basil agreed that Christians must free themselves from loving their stuff so much, but he also knew that Christians must follow Christ's commandment to love their neighbor as themselves. By giving our possessions to the poor, we show them love, and this is truly Christ's greatest commandment.

Saint Basil famously said, "The bread you are holding back is for the hungry, the clothes you keep put away are for the naked, the shoes that are rotting away with disuse are for those who have none, the silver you keep buried in the earth is for the needy." In other words, if there is extra food in your pantry or extra stuff in your house, then you are supposed to give it to the poor. Stop holding onto their stuff and spread it around.

Saint Basil's love for the sick and the poor led him to establish the very first hospital, which was called New City. There, Christians could show true love to those who needed it: they could care for the poor, the aging, and the sick, feeding them and spending time with them, just as Christ calls us to do. The New City was meant to be an icon of the Kingdom of God, a little glimpse of heaven. Saint Basil was right there in the midst of it, a spiritual leader and a doctor himself, treating everyone for free and offering hugs, prayers, and love.

Pray for us, St. John Climacus and St. Basil the Great, as we learn to renounce money and possessions and to love only God and our neighbors!

ᗞ

The rich young ruler wanted to know what more he could do to attain eternal life. What did Jesus say?

"Sell everything you have and give to the poor, and you will have treasure in heaven. Then come, follow Me."

Why would it be hard for rich people to enter the Kingdom of heaven?

Because they have so many possessions that they love, and it's hard not to love those things more than you love God.

What kind of institution did St. Basil the Great build to help him love his neighbors?

He built the first hospital, and Christians gave money and time to help take care of the poor and needy.

FOR DISCUSSION: Do you have stuff that would be hard to give away? Can you imagine what it would feel like to be non-possessive? When people experience a disaster—perhaps a fire or a hurricane—and lose their stuff, what are they usually grateful for? How can we remind ourselves to focus our love on people and not stuff?

The Fifth Wednesday of Great Lent

As we consider St. John's *Ladder* and explore the Lenten theme of almsgiving, let's take some time to look at a time when our Lord saw a widow with two little coins (called mites), and what He taught about her gift to the temple.

In chapter 21 of the Gospel of St. Luke, we read:

And He looked up and saw the rich putting their gifts into the treasury, and He saw also a certain poor widow putting in two mites. So He said, "Truly I say to you that this poor widow has put in more than all; for all these out of their abundance have put in offerings for God, but she out of her poverty put in all the livelihood that she had." (Luke 21:1–4)

We notice that Jesus is watching the people as they put their gifts into the treasury at the temple. He notices what we do with our money as well—how much we give to the poor, to those in need, and to His holy Church. He pays attention to these things because they are important.

Christ sees that the rich are putting their gifts into the treasury, and we can assume that these are generous gifts; the rich are able to offer large amounts of money for the temple treasury.

A poor widow approaches and offers just two mites—a tiny sum, far less than what the rich have offered.

And yet, our Lord has a different view on it. He says that "this poor widow has put in more than all" because she "put in all the livelihood that she had." The rich people can give large gifts and still have plenty left for themselves, but this widow's tiny gift was everything she had, so it meant more to our Lord.

The Fathers would say that the Lord measures the value of our gifts not by how much is given, but by how much we hold back for ourselves.

In so many ways, God wants all of us. He wants all of our heart, all of our soul. So when we give what might look to others to be a nice, generous gift, God knows if we have held more than we needed. He knows if we are giving with our whole hearts.

If we can truly trust that God will take care of us, we can share everything we have with others and trust that God will send more. Abba Dorotheos said,

> *No one can say, "I am poor and hence I have no means of giving alms." For even if you cannot give as the rich gave their gifts into the temple treasury, give two farthings as the poor widow did, and from you God will consider it a greater gift than the gifts of the rich. And if you do not have as much as two farthings? You can take pity on the sick and give alms by ministering to them. And if you cannot do even this? You can comfort your brother by your words. "A good word is better than the best of gifts."*

So even if we have only a very small amount of money, giving even two tiny coins is truly a great gift. And even more importantly, Abba Dorotheos reminds us that almsgiving is not just about money—we are asked to give what we have. If we have money, we should give it. If we have time and love, we can give those. We should be generous with our love and our talents and our blessings. We should do what we can to be helpful to others, because what God wants to see is not really about money, but about love. God wants to see that we love one another as we love ourselves. He wants us to take care of other people as we take care of ourselves. It's not about giving a *lot* of money but about giving what we have.

Saint John Chrysostom once said,

The amount we give is not judged by the largeness of the gifts but the largeness of our hearts. The poor woman who shares her meager pot of stew with another poor woman is far more to be praised than the rich man who throws a few gold coins into a collection at church. But although most Christians acknowledge the truth of this, their words and actions convey a different message. When a rich man makes a large gift to the church, he is heartily thanked; and although he will not feel the lack of that money himself, he is praised for his generosity. When a poor man makes a small gift, nothing is said. Even though that gift may cause him to go hungry, no one praises him or thanks him. It would be better to praise no one than to confine our praise to the rich. Better still, we should take trouble to observe every true act of generosity, whether by the rich or the poor, and then offer our praise. Indeed, let us be as generous with our praise as people are generous with their money.

During this Lenten season, let's work on being generous—not just with money, but with praise and with love and with our time and attention.

⤜

The rich people gave a lot of money, and then a little widow came along. How much did she give?

Only two mites, which is not very much.

Jesus said that she gave more than the others. Why?

The others kept back enough money to live very well, but she did not keep anything back —she gave everything she had.

If you don't have any money, can you still give? What can you give?

You can give your time and attention and your love. You have talents and blessings you can share with others.

FOR DISCUSSION: Is there someone you could visit and spend time with, who would really appreciate it? Maybe a neighbor or family member? Maybe a nursing home nearby? Does that feel like giving alms or sacrificing something out of love for someone else? Think of ways you could give to someone.

The Fifth Thursday of Great Lent

A S WE CONSIDER THE LENTEN theme of almsgiving, we might look to the modern saint Nikolai Velimirovich and think about some wonderful stories he told about giving alms to the poor.

For example, in his huge collection of all the saints' lives called *The Prologue of Ohrid*, St. Nikolai reminds us that the Lord said, "Assuredly, I say unto you, inasmuch as you did *it* to one of the least of these My brethren, you did *it* to Me" (Matt. 25:40).

Saint Nikolai begins by reminding us that when we give to the poor, we are giving to Jesus. When we offer a drink or a blanket or a smile to the least of these, then Jesus considers this a gift to Him. That makes sense, because every person is an icon of Christ. If we kiss an icon of Jesus, we know that we're really kissing Jesus. So if a person is an icon of Jesus, and that person is in need, then when we give help to that person, we are really helping Jesus.

Saint Nikolai continues, "Similar things happen in almsgiving and in Holy Communion. In Holy Communion we receive the Living Lord Christ Himself, in the form of bread and wine; in almsgiving we give to the Living Lord Christ Himself, in the form of the poor and needy."

This is a great mystery, just like Holy Communion. Just as you can receive Jesus Christ right there in church, you can also meet Him on the street in the body of a poor person. Miraculously and mysteriously, Jesus can be present in bread and wine, and He can be present in other human beings so that you can interact with Him right here in our world.

Then St. Nikolai tells an interesting story:

> A certain man in Constantinople was unusually merciful. Walking along the streets of the city, he would press his gift into the hands of the poor and hurry onward so he would not hear their gratitude or be recognized. When a friend of his asked how he had become so merciful, he replied: "Once in church I heard a priest say that whoever gives to the poor gives into the hands of Christ Himself. I didn't believe it, for I thought, 'How can this be, when Christ is in heaven?' However, I was on my way home one day and I saw a poor man begging, and the face of Christ shone above his head! Just then a passerby gave the beggar a piece of bread, and I saw the Lord extend His hand, take the bread, and bless the donor. From then on, I have always seen Christ's face shining above the beggars. Therefore, with great fear I perform as much charity as I can." (Reflection for September 18, The Prologue of Ohrid, Volume II)

God sent this man a vision so that he could understand that it really is true that when we give to the least of these, we are truly giving to Christ—that what is given to the icon of Christ passes to the real Christ.

Think of how amazing this is! Those of us who were not alive when our Lord Jesus Christ walked on the earth in His human body have a new chance to offer Him worship and love, clothing and food and drink and money, every time we see someone in need. So many people in the Bible had the opportunity to eat a meal with Jesus—and so do we, whenever we are willing to sit down and spend time with someone in need.

Of course, when we see someone begging on the street, we don't always think kind and compassionate thoughts. Some people will find themselves annoyed with too many requests for money, for food, for help. But the ones in need are the least of these. If we can love them, we are loving Jesus—and yet, we don't always feel loving. What do we do when our hearts just aren't reaching back with compassion?

Saint Nikolai tells us:

> *Do not ever say: "These beggars annoy me!" So many millions of men live on earth and all are beggars before the Lord; emperors as well as laborers, the wealthy as well as servants, all are beggars before the Lord, and the Lord never said: "These beggars annoy me!"*

If we can remember that we are truly beggars before the Lord, that we have not earned any of our blessings but that we ask endlessly for more, then perhaps we can find some patience and love for the beggars who surround us. After all, we are all beggars.

Saint Nikolai had so many wonderful ways to help us understand the ways of the Lord. He was so well loved that another famous saint, St. John Maximovitch, called him a great saint and Chrysostom of our day. He was a great scholar and thinker and the Serbian Orthodox Bishop of Zicha. Though he was a Serbian bishop, he spent a lot of time in America. In fact, his final years were all spent in America, and he died here and was buried here for a long time. Today, his body is back in Serbia, but he is well loved in both countries.

You will probably not be surprised to hear that St. Nikolai was wonderful at almsgiving. In his own village of Lelich, he built a beautiful church, and just like the holy apostles, he kept nothing. Much wealth came into his hands, only to pass right through them; he handed it off to places with trouble or tears or orphans needing love and support. He kept nothing for himself, like the widow with two mites.

Pray for us, St. Nikolai!

ॐ

If people are icons of Christ, what does it mean when we are helping a person in need?

Just as our veneration passes from the icon to the person it depicts, our help and the love we give pass from the person receiving our help to Jesus Himself.

How does this reflect the mystery of Holy Communion?

As Jesus is mysteriously present in the bread and wine, He is mysteriously present in other human beings.

What is a helpful thought when we are annoyed by people always asking for money or time from us?

We are also beggars before the Lord. We cannot really deserve anything, so everything we have is a gift from God, and we are always begging Him for more blessings.

FOR DISCUSSION: If human beings are icons of Christ, then everything we offer them we offer to Christ—whether that is food or drink, love or comfort. Does that mean that bad things we do to other people are also being done to Christ? How does that idea make you think about your own behavior?

The Fifth Friday of Great Lent

A S WE CONSIDER THE IMPORTANCE of almsgiving, we turn to a lesson Jesus teaches us about how giving alms is really part of our very salvation. In the Gospel of Luke, chapter 16, we read:

There was a certain rich man who was clothed in purple and fine linen and fared sumptuously every day. But there was a certain beggar named Lazarus, full of sores, who was laid at his gate, desiring to be fed with the crumbs which fell from the rich man's table. Moreover the dogs came and licked his sores. So it was that the beggar died, and was carried by the angels to Abraham's bosom. The rich man also died and was buried. And being in torments in Hades, he lifted up his eyes and saw Abraham afar off, and Lazarus in his bosom.

Then he cried and said, "Father Abraham, have mercy on me, and send Lazarus that he may dip the tip of his finger in water and cool my tongue; for I am tormented in this flame." But Abraham said, "Son, remember that in your lifetime you received your good things, and likewise Lazarus evil things; but now he is comforted and you are tormented. And besides all this, between us and you there is a great gulf fixed, so that those who want to pass from here to you cannot, nor can those from there pass to us."

Then he said, "I beg you therefore, father, that you would send him to my father's house, for I have five brothers, that he may testify to them, lest they also come to this place of torment." Abraham said to him, "They have Moses and the prophets; let them hear them." And he said, "No, father Abraham; but if one goes to them from the dead, they will repent." But he said to him, "If they do not hear Moses and the prophets, neither will they be persuaded though one rise from the dead." (Luke 16:19–31)

The Church Fathers tell us that God put the beggar Lazarus on the rich man's doorstep for a reason: He was giving this hard-hearted rich man an opportunity to show love. Every day, this poor man named Lazarus lay in his way as he walked out his door—every day, the rich man stepped right over him and kept walking. God was giving the rich man chance after chance to show love to an unfortunate soul, and he refused every time.

Saint John Chrysostom said, "The rich exist for the sake of the poor. The poor exist for the salvation of the rich." What could he mean by that? God sends riches to some people for the sake of the poor—that is, God gives them more than they need so that they will have enough to share with the poor. At the same time, the poor exist for the salvation of the rich—by being icons of Christ in need, they give the rich an opportunity to choose to love God more than they love material things, to share their abundance and love their neighbors. Almsgiving is good because it feeds the poor, but it is also good for the soul of the rich person.

There are plenty of examples of rich people in the Scriptures who go to heaven. For example, we remember Righteous Joseph in Egypt, who had great riches and power at his disposal, and he used them to save his family and all of Israel from starving. Similarly, Joseph of Arimathea was a righteous and rich man, and he gave his own tomb to Jesus Christ. The Pharisee Nicodemus was wealthy enough to buy many bottles of expensive oil to anoint Christ's body. Each of these rich men was righteous. They loved God and were happy to share their wealth with those in need and with God. Their riches became one way they showed love and generosity to God and to the people God sent into their lives.

It is not impossible for a rich person to be saved—with God, anything is possible. But it is important that those who have been blessed with riches should be generous. God wanted the rich man in this parable to be saved, and He sent Lazarus to help. We must keep our eyes open for the people God places in our path. We must offer them love, whether that is a meal or money or just some company and a smile.

༄

Did the rich man in this story share his riches with others?

No. A man named Lazarus lay on his doorstep every day, but the man just stepped over him.

When the two men die, which one is with Abraham in the good part of Hades, and which one is suffering there?

Lazarus is with Abraham, and the rich man is in flames.

Why did God put Lazarus on that doorstep every day?

God was trying to save the rich man by offering him a perfect opportunity to show love.

FOR DISCUSSION: At the end of the parable, the rich man wants to send Lazarus to warn his brothers that they must not be hard-hearted, or they will end up like him. Abraham says to the rich man, "If they do not hear Moses and the prophets, neither will they be persuaded though one rise from the dead." We know another Lazarus will rise from the dead, and then Christ will rise from the dead. Will everyone listen to His message then? Will they begin to obey, or will some people still be greedy and cold and have no love for others?

The Fifth Saturday of Great Lent

A S WE FINISH THIS WEEK'S look at almsgiving, let's consider ways you might give alms that don't involve money.

In the Book of the Acts of the Apostles, which is the story of what the apostles did after Christ's death and Resurrection, we read about a man who was asking for alms:

> Now Peter and John went up together to the temple at the hour of prayer, the ninth hour. And a certain man lame from his mother's womb was carried, whom they laid daily at the gate of the temple which is called Beautiful, to ask alms from those who entered the temple; who, seeing Peter and John about to go into the temple, asked for alms. And fixing his eyes on him, with John, Peter said, "Look at us." So he gave them his attention, expecting to receive something from them. Then Peter said, "Silver and gold I do not have, but what I do have I give you: In the name of Jesus Christ of Nazareth, rise up and walk." And he took him by the right hand and lifted him up, and immediately his feet and ankle bones received strength. So he, leaping up, stood and walked and entered the temple with them—walking, leaping, and praising God. (Acts 3:1–8)

Every day, people helped this man who could not walk by setting him in the doorway of the temple so that he could ask for alms. When he saw Peter and John, he asked them for money, but the apostles didn't carry money. They owned very little and traveled around with just the clothes on their backs. They had no silver or gold to offer him, but they did have a much more important and profound gift to give this man: they offered him healing in the name of Jesus Christ.

The paralytic man asked for money, but money wasn't really what he needed. Sure, he needed to find his next meal, but truly, he needed the healing power of Jesus Christ—both physically and spiritually.

This is true for all of us. We may ask one another for money or food, and we do need those things, but all human beings have a need for healing, and whether we know it or not, we need the love of Jesus Christ to be made whole. You and I may not be able to call down a miraculous healing, but we can share love with other human beings and show them a glimpse of what Jesus is like by loving and helping them.

There are many healing saints who could heal people miraculously and also through medical interventions. There are many doctor saints, and many of them are called unmercenary healers, which means that they treated patients without charging money. This was their service to God, through the people He put in their path.

One such saint is St. Luke the Surgeon, who was born in 1877. His father was Catholic and his mother was Orthodox, and they baptized him with the name Valentin. His parents raised their children to love and serve God by serving others. Although they were not rich, his mother often took food to prisoners, and his father (who was a pharmacist) would prepare medicine for the sick. Being raised in an environment like this had a powerful effect on Valentin.

Valentin was a talented artist and considered becoming a painter, but he decided instead to study medicine so that he could help more poor people. When he realized how many poor people were struggling with blindness, he began studying how to treat eyes, and he cared for patients in his family's home. He would not accept any pay from his patients, and while he was in school he studied both the sciences and the Scriptures.

When Valentin was forty, the Bolshevik Revolution began. Life became difficult for Christians in that part of the world. Valentin and his wife and children moved to Tashkent, where he became the surgeon in one of the biggest hospitals in the country. It was a dangerous time for everyone: even the hospital had bullet holes in it, and Valentin often risked his life while he was working to save the lives of others. During this time in Tashkent, his wife, Anna, became ill with tuberculosis and passed away. Their children were aged six to twelve. Valentin prayed that God would provide for the children's needs and help him to raise them. God answered by sending a nurse named Soa, who loved Valentin's children so much that she became a second mother to them (even raising them and sending them to school in later years, when Valentin was unable to care for them).

Valentin's deep faith lead him to always keep an icon of the Theotokos in his surgery room. He prayed before every operation, marking the patient with an iodine cross at the location where the operation was to be done. At one point, when the Soviets took control of Tashkent, they removed the icon—but Valentin refused to do surgery without it. Soon the wife of one of the military leaders was in serious condition and needed an operation. They requested that Valentin do it, because he was known to be the best surgeon in Russia. He refused to operate on the woman without the icon on the wall, and before long, the icon was put back in its place on the wall of the surgery room. Valentin saved the woman's life, with the help of the Theotokos.

Although it was a dangerous time to be related in any way to the Church, Valentin became a priest in 1921. He continued to work as a doctor, also directing a hospital and teaching anatomy, all while dressed as an Orthodox priest, which irritated the authorities in Tashkent. In 1923, Fr. Valentin was secretly ordained a bishop and was given the name of Luke. Within a month, he was exiled for his role in the Church.

Over the next eleven years, the government would send Bishop Luke away many times, often to Siberia and other difficult places to live, because of his faith. No matter where he was sent, the people were glad to see him. He would serve them as a bishop in whatever spaces they could manage to meet: whether on a riverbank or in a small cottage, he would lead the Divine Liturgy and other services and encourage people to follow God. He also would help as a doctor whenever possible, healing people's bodies as well as their souls.

One of the most difficult things for Bishop Luke was being so far from his children during this time. They wrote letters to each other, and Bishop Luke prayed for them intensely. God healed the children when they were ill, even though their doctor father was not around, simply through Bishop Luke's prayers. Over the years, God brought other children into Bishop Luke's life, and he cared for them as if they were his own. All the young people under his care greatly benefited from their interaction with the bishop, and (among other things) he taught them that the most important thing in life is always to do good—even when you cannot do much to help others, try to do even the smallest good thing.

Bishop Luke always tried to do good for others. Whether he was a prisoner giving away his coat to another prisoner, or as an old man working day and night, or serving the liturgy at a church an hour and a half's walk away over slippery roads, he did everything he could to help others. Even at the age of seventy, when he was transferred to Simferopol in Crimea, he still wanted to serve others. There was only one church left in all of Crimea when Archbishop Luke arrived there. The people were very poor, and they were starving, but in spite of all these challenges, Archbishop Luke helped the people. By the time he finished, there were more than sixty churches there.

At age seventy-four, Archbishop Luke went completely blind. However, he was able to continue serving. God's guidance, as well as his years of experience as a surgeon, made him able to be so precise in his service that people who didn't know he was blind could not tell that he was. Despite this new challenge of blindness, Archbishop Luke continued to serve sick people by praying for them. (For example, a young girl named Galina, who had a brain tumor, was healed by his prayers. She later went on to become a doctor to help others.)

After he became blind, Archbishop Luke's granddaughter Vera came to help him. She would cook a big pot of food every day in their apartment. The poor, children, and elderly would come to the apartment, looking for the food. Although he ate only once a day, Archbishop Luke would ask each evening if there had been enough for the others who had come for the other meals. He would not allow Vera to purchase new clothes for him. Instead, he always asked her to mend his old ones because "there are many poor people around." His concern was never for himself, but for others, to the day that he fell asleep in the Lord on June 11, 1961, at eighty-four years of age.

Saint Luke's life shows us that there are many ways to serve the poor, whether by providing money or food or shelter, or, most profoundly, by offering them the healing power of Jesus Christ.

Pray for us, St. Luke!

ॐ

The apostles refused to give a paralytic beggar money when he asked for it. Why?

They did not have any money, but they gave him what they had: the healing of Jesus Christ.

Why did Valentin decide not to become an artist?

He really wanted to help poor people, so he became a doctor for the peasants of Russia.

Valentin (or St. Luke) was frequently sent away by the Soviet government to desolate places like the far reaches of Siberia. Why?

Because he was a Christian who would not hide his faith or give it up.

FOR DISCUSSION: Saint Luke became a great surgeon so that he could serve the poor with his abilities. At the same time, he was an Orthodox bishop. Do you think that it would be hard to know whether he saved you with his medical skills or with his prayers? Does God do miracles through doctors?

The Sunday of St. Mary of Egypt

TODAY WE CELEBRATE ST. MARY of Egypt, who is a great saint but whose life was not always saintly. That's why she is such a favorite in the Church, actually—she is a wonderful example of how we can turn our lives around when we truly repent.

What we know about St. Mary actually comes to us through a monk named St. Zosimas. He lived in a monastery as a child and then stayed to become a monk as an adult, and by the time he was fifty-three years old, he was very holy. He was so holy that he had a hard time finding a teacher holier than he was. He prayed that God might show one to him. Suddenly, an angel appeared and told him to travel to a monastery near the Jordan River.

Abba Zosimas immediately left for the Jordan Monastery and settled in. (*Abba* means "Father," and Zosimas was a priest, so we call him Abba Zosimas.) He met many wonderful elders there at the monastery and saw that they sang constantly and prayed all night long. Soon, Great Lent arrived, and this particular monastery had an interesting custom: on the first Sunday of Great Lent, they all received Holy Communion at the Divine Liturgy, and then they did a forgiveness service, making prostrations and asking each other for forgiveness. And then they opened the monastery gate and went off into the wilderness. Each monk took some food and went into the desert. When their food ran out, they ate roots and desert plants. The monks all crossed the Jordan River, but then they scattered in various directions so that no one might see how another fasted or how they spent their time. They would meet again at the monastery on Palm Sunday.

So when Great Lent began, Abba Zosimas went deep into the desert, hoping to find a teacher there. He walked for twenty days, singing and praying, and finally he saw a human form—but he was afraid, thinking that it might be a demon. Then he crossed himself with the sign of the cross, and he felt better. He turned and saw that it was a person whose faded short hair was white like a sheep's fleece. Abba Zosimas rejoiced, since he had not seen any living thing for many days. The desert-dweller saw Zosimas and tried to run, but Abba Zosimas hurried after.

The stranger said to him, "Forgive me, Abba Zosimas, but I cannot turn and show my face to you. I am a woman, and as you see, I am not wearing clothes. If you would grant the request of a sinful woman, throw me your cloak so I might cover my body, and then I can ask for your blessing."

Then Abba Zosimas knew she was holy, because she knew his name. He threw her his cloak, and they spoke together and prayed together for a while. She knew all about him—that he was a priest and a monk, looking to learn something. When she prayed, she raised her hands and whispered so softly that Abba Zosimas could not make out her words—and then she rose into the air more than a foot above the ground. Seeing this, Zosimas threw himself down on the ground, weeping and repeating, "Lord, have mercy!"

Saint Zosimas asked about her life, and she replied, "It distresses me, Father, to speak to you about my shameless life. When you hear my story, you might flee from me, as if I were a poisonous snake. But I shall tell you everything, Father."

She explained that she was born in Egypt, and when she was twelve years old, she ran away from her parents and went to Alexandria, where she lived a shameful life but felt no shame. She loved wild parties and behaving badly, and she spent her time with every sinful person she could find. She had a great thirst for wine and sin and spent seventeen years pursuing pleasure. One summer, she saw that a group of pilgrims were heading across the sea to Jerusalem for the Feast of the Exaltation of the Holy Cross. To her, this seemed like a big party and a challenge to distract some Christians from their Faith, so she joined them on a boat to Jerusalem.

God had other plans for Mary, and when the day of the feast arrived, everything changed for her.

When the other pilgrims headed to the church for the feast, Mary went along with them. She walked up to the doors and tried to squeeze into the church. Although she stepped up to the threshold, a force held her back, preventing her from entering. She tried again and again to enter, but every time—somehow the way the crowd moved just pushed her out, or a strange, invisible force kept her away—she could not pass through the church door. As she stood before the door, she realized that her sins were keeping her outside, and she began to cry. She saw an icon of the Holy Theotokos and cried out to her for help. She declared herself unworthy but begged the Theotokos to help her to become worthy. She promised to change, to repent of all her sins, and to begin a whole new life. The Theotokos helped her, and she entered the church.

After venerating the cross, she fell to the ground and kissed it, and then she went back outside to the icon and thanked the Holy Theotokos for helping her. She promised to keep her vow and asked the Theotokos to guide her on the path of her repentance.

Then Mary heard a voice from on high: "If you cross the Jordan River, you will find glorious rest."

The Holy Theotokos was guiding her. As Mary left the church, a man handed her three coins, and she went to buy some bread, asking the baker the way to the Jordan River. Mary stayed out in the desert, on the other side of the Jordan, for forty-seven years without seeing another soul. When she had finished her bread, she ate what she found in the desert, fasting like St. John the Forerunner.

Mary said that the first seventeen years were the hardest as she struggled with thirst and hunger. The old, obnoxious drunken songs she used to sing would still ring in her ears, and she struggled with them, trying to replace their ugliness with beautiful prayer. It was really hard for her to get those songs out of her head and to fight all of the desires for the sinful activities of her youth. She would struggle and fight, throwing herself onto the ground in tears, until God would send a blessed light that would encircle her and give her peace. After seventeen years, the peace won, and she was able to live joyfully with the help of the Mother of God.

We will talk more about Mary and Zosimas tomorrow, but for now, let's just stop and think about what an amazing story this is. The Church especially loves St. Mary of Egypt because she had loved sin so much, and yet she dedicated herself to God and overcame all her wild passions. Mary was very sinful, and yet God loved her enough to block her from entering that church until she understood that it was time to repent. Sometimes welcoming us home means locking us out. God does what it takes to reach us and to call us home.

What interesting Lenten custom did the Jordan monastery follow?

On Forgiveness Sunday, the monks went to Divine Liturgy and asked each other's forgiveness. Then each monk went out into the wilderness alone for forty days.

How did Abba Zosimas know that Mary was very holy?

She knew his name without him telling her, and when she prayed, she rose up off the ground.

What made Mary realize that she should repent and change her life?

When she could not enter the church with the rest of the people, she recognized that her sins kept her outside, and she cried tears of repentance. She asked the Theotokos to help her make this tremendous change in her life.

FOR DISCUSSION: Why does the Church bring our attention to St. Mary of Egypt here at the close of Great Lent? Now that we have been fasting and praying and giving alms, perhaps our hearts are ready to see our own sins, as Mary suddenly saw hers. Mary did not accomplish her repentance in the desert alone. Who helped her? Who can help us?

The Sixth Monday of Great Lent

A S WE RECALL, ABBA ZOSIMAS was a very holy monk who hoped to find a teacher who could help him grow holier. An angel led him to the Jordan monastery, where the monks spent Great Lent alone in the wilderness. After twenty days out in the desert alone, he met a wild-looking person who knew his name and rose up into the air when she prayed. She told him the story of her life—how she had been an unusually sinful young woman, truly loving sin and giving her entire self over to it. But in Jerusalem, at the Feast of the Exaltation of the Cross, she realized that she was sinful and decided to make a change with the help of the Holy Theotokos. For seventeen years she struggled, but since then she had lived in peace and in prayer out in the desert.

As she spoke to Abba Zosimas, she kept quoting the Scriptures; the monk recognized the words and phrases she would use from the Psalms, from the books written by Moses, and the book of Job. He was confused: surely in her wild youth she had not studied the Scriptures? He asked, "Mother, have you read the Psalms and other books?"

She smiled at his question and answered, "Believe me, I have seen no human face but yours from the time that I crossed over the Jordan. I never learned from books. I have never heard anyone read or sing from them. Perhaps the Word of God, which is alive and acting, teaches man knowledge directly."

Mary had been alone in the desert, but she was not alone. The Holy Theotokos was comforting her and giving her strength, and the Word of God (perhaps our Lord Jesus Christ, or the Holy Spirit) was teaching her.

Mary told Abba Zosimas not to tell anyone about her until she died, and she sent him back to the monastery with a request. She asked him not to cross the Jordan at Great Lent the next year. She said, "Remain at the monastery. Even if you try to leave the monastery, you will not be able to do so. On Great and Holy Thursday, the day of the Lord's Last Supper, place the Life-Creating Body and Blood of Christ our God in a holy vessel, and bring it to me. Await me on this side of the Jordan, at the edge of the desert, so that I may receive the Holy Mysteries."

Asking for his prayers, the woman turned and vanished into the depths of the desert. For a whole year Abba Zosimas remained silent, not daring to reveal to anyone what he had seen, and he prayed that the Lord would grant him to see the holy ascetic once more.

When the first week of Great Lent came again, Saint Zosimas fell ill and could not join the other monks out in the wilderness. Then he remembered Mary's prediction that he would not be able to leave the monastery. After several days went by, Saint Zosimas was well again, but he waited at the monastery until Holy Week.

On Holy Thursday, Abba Zosimas did what he had promised: he placed some of the Body and Blood of Christ into a chalice and went to the Jordan River to wait for Mary. The saint seemed tardy, and Abba Zosimas prayed that God would permit him to see the holy woman.

Finally, he saw her standing on the far side of the river. Rejoicing, St. Zosimas got up and glorified God—and then he wondered how she could cross the Jordan without a boat. She made the sign of the cross over the water, then she walked on the water and crossed the Jordan River. Abba Zosimas saw her in the moonlight, walking toward him on the water, and was amazed. When she reached the shore, she said to Abba Zosimas, "Bless me, Father." Together, they recited the Creed and the Our Father, and then she received Holy Communion and raised her hands to the heavens, saying, "Lord, now let Your servant depart in peace, for my eyes have seen Your salvation."

Mary sent Abba Zosimas back to the monastery again, asking him to come back in one year to the place where they first spoke. Again she made the sign of the cross over the Jordan River, walked over the water, and disappeared into the desert. Abba Zosimas returned to the monastery.

The next year, Abba Zosimas went into the desert. He reached the place where he first saw the holy woman ascetic and found her body lying there, with her arms folded on her bosom. Abba Zosimas washed her feet with his tears and kissed them. For a long while he wept over her, sang the Psalms, and said the funeral prayers. He began to wonder whether the saint would want him to bury her or not. Suddenly, he saw something written on the ground near her head: "Abba Zosimas, bury on this spot the body of humble Mary. Return to dust what is dust. Pray to the Lord for me. I reposed on the first day of April, on the very night of the saving Passion of Christ, after partaking of the Mystical Supper."

Reading this note, Abba Zosimas was glad to learn her name. He then realized that St. Mary, after receiving the Holy Mysteries from his hand on Holy Thursday, had died in this spot. This was amazing because it had taken him twenty days to walk all the way there, but she had travelled there very quickly—maybe even miraculously. Abba Zosimas was amazed and glorified God.

But then Abba Zosimas realized that he had no shovel. He

picked up a small piece of wood and began to dig. The ground was hard and dry, and he could not dig it. Looking up, suddenly Abba Zosimas saw an enormous lion. It was standing by the saint's body and licking her feet. The elder was terrified; he crossed himself and asked for Mary's prayers. Then the lion, moving in a friendly and relaxed way, came closer, and Abba Zosimas commanded the lion to dig the grave. Immediately, the lion dug a hole deep enough to bury St. Mary, and then the lion just went back into the desert. Abba Zosimas buried the holy woman and returned to the monastery, blessing and praising Christ our God.

When he got back to the monastery, Abba Zosimas told everyone the story of St. Mary of Egypt, and they were amazed. They would always remember St. Mary, and they prayed for her and asked her to pray for them.

Abba Zosimas had grown up as a child in the monastery and became a monk as soon as he could. He did not have a wild youth, and he became a very holy man. And yet God showed him that a woman with a completely wild life, with her heart entirely given over to sinfulness, could truly repent and become the holiest of people. This means that it is never too late. No matter what kind of life we are living, we can truly repent, and God will help us. While some saints are simply saintly from their birth, others spend years of their lives in sin and do terrible things. But God loves the sinners too, and He will help us in our struggles if we repent.

Every year during Great Lent, we take some time to fast (and even if it's not a fast in the desert like Mary's, it can be hard to do) and to overcome our sinfulness. We cannot do it alone, but with God anything is possible.

☙

When Mary spoke, she used phrases and words that are in the Scriptures, though she never studied the Scriptures. How did she learn them?

She said that perhaps the Word of God taught her, out there in the desert.

What did Mary want Abba Zosimas to bring her from the monastery?

She asked him to wait for Holy Thursday then bring her Holy Communion.

Abba Zosimas could not dig a hole to bury Mary. Who dug it for him?

A lion came and obediently dug the hole.

FOR DISCUSSION: Many great saints have a wonderful relationship with animals. Animals are God's creation, and they obey Him, so it can be a sign of great holiness when animals are gentle and obedient with the saints. (We might think of Daniel in the lion's den, or of St. Herman and the bears in Alaska.) So the lion's arrival to bury Mary is considered another sign of her great holiness. Why does God provide so many signs? Why was it important for Abba Zosimas and for us to know that Mary was so holy? How does this help us?

The Sixth Tuesday of Great Lent

WE BEGAN THIS WEEK WITH the story of St. Mary of Egypt, whose repentance led her to spend forty-seven years fasting in the desert. This week, in her honor, we'll explore the Lenten theme of fasting.

Saint John Chrysostom said, "Fasting is wonderful, because it tramples our sins like a dirty weed while it cultivates and raises truth like a flower." We can see this in St. Mary of Egypt's life: when she was young, she loved to sin, but in the desert her fasting trampled her sins and grew holiness like a wonderful flower in her heart. Fasting is really how we tend the garden of our hearts, tearing out the spiritual weeds of sin and nurturing the sweetly fragrant flowers of a healthy spiritual life.

Have you ever heard the saying, "What comes out of your mouth is more important than what goes in"?

Generally, when we talk about fasting we are usually talking about what goes into our mouth—food. We mean that we'll avoid meat and dairy products in our diet, depending on our health and medical situation. Eating a vegan diet is simply changing what we eat. But going on a diet won't make you holy. In fact, if you are great at eating only Lenten foods but then you spend your time yelling at people and calling them names, then you aren't becoming holier at all. What comes out of your mouth is more important than what you put in it.

Fasting is really not just a change in diet, but a whole change in our behavior and our outlook. The discipline in our diet should be matched by discipline in the rest of our lives as we try to be the best Orthodox Christians we can be during the fast. We pray more, we go to church more often, we study God's Word more. But fasting also means doing some things less—arguing less, being less angry, being less stingy.

This is what St. John Chrysostom says about fasting:

Fasting is the change of every part of our life. [. . .] Are you fasting? Show me your fast with your works. Which works? If you see someone who is poor, show him mercy. If you see an enemy, reconcile with him. If you see a friend who is becoming successful, do not be jealous of him! If you see a beautiful woman on the street, pass her by.

In other words, not only should the mouth fast, but the eyes and the legs and the arms and all the other parts of the body should fast as well. Let the hands fast, remaining clean from stealing and greediness. Let the legs fast, avoiding roads which lead to sinful sights. Let the eyes fast by not fixing themselves on beautiful faces and by not observing the beauty of others. (On Fasting)

Our whole body can fast. Fasting is so much more than being careful about what kinds of foods we eat. It's really about being careful about everything—what we hear, what we do, where we go. We need to be fasting in all of our actions. St. John continues,

Let the mouth fast from disgraceful and abusive words, because what gain is there when, on the one hand we avoid eating chicken and fish and, on the other, we chew up and consume our brothers? He who condemns and blasphemes is as if he has eaten brotherly meat, as if he has bitten into the flesh of his fellow man.

What an amazing thing to say! Here we are fasting from meat, but if we are yelling insults or gossiping nastily, it's as if we were biting into our brother. How much better if we were to eat a hamburger rather than "eat" our brothers and sisters!

Saint John is not saying that we should *not* fast from meat, but that we should *also* fast from being mean. He is saying that if all you're doing is eating a vegan diet, then you're not really going to grow holier. We will only see ourselves grow holier and closer to God if we are really trying to live by His commandment to love one another as we love ourselves. If we are not working on living better, more Christian lives, then we aren't really fasting.

The food part of fasting really is important. We started out our Lenten meditations with the Fall of Adam and Eve in the garden. Right from the beginning in Paradise, people were supposed to fast. God gave Adam and Eve one rule: "Of the tree of the knowledge of good and evil you shall not eat." Their failure to follow that rule is a failure to fast properly, and it ushered in sin and death to our world. Learning to control our appetites is a big step on the way back to Paradise.

The food part of fasting is a tool that we use to help us grow closer to God.

Consider this saying from St. Seraphim of Sarov: "One should not think about the doings of God when one's stomach is full; on a full stomach there can be no vision of the divine mysteries." ("The Spiritual Instructions to Laymen and Monks," printed in *Little Russian Philokalia: St. Seraphim of Sarov*)

When we fast from heavy and rich foods, like meat and dairy products, we become more awake to prayer. We get a little bit lazy and tired when we are well fed, but when we are eating smaller, lighter meals, our minds and our hearts are more open and ready to understand and to receive God. That's really why we fast—to make ourselves better at praying, better at feeling God's presence.

So during Great Lent and the other fasting periods of the year, we want to increase some things (like praying, doing good deeds, and showing love for others), and we want to decrease other things (like eating so much heavy food, arguing and getting angry, feasting on our brothers). We follow the example of St. Mary of Egypt, who ate less and prayed more. She defeated sinfulness with prayerfulness and fasting, and God will help all of us do that if we show up with our best efforts every Lent.

As we get closer to Holy Week, now is a good time to ask ourselves how our fasting is going this year. If there are changes or adjustments we need to make, we still have time.

჻

When we think of Great Lent, we think of fasting from food, but St. John Chrysostom says there's more to do. What should we do more of during Great Lent?

We should do more good things—we should pray more, we should take care of the hungry and sick, and we should practice loving our neighbors even more.

What should we do less of during Great Lent?

We should stop arguing and bickering and being greedy. We should stop doing the sinful things that keep us away from God.

Why do we want to eat less of the heavy, rich foods during Great Lent?

Because it is hard to pray and to receive God on a full stomach, but it is easier on a lighter stomach.

For Discussion: Have you noticed yourself having trouble controlling your anger or frustrations during Great Lent? What could you do the help that? And if you are fasting, do you notice a difference in your prayer life? Think about that now, and then think about it again after Pascha, when you've taken a break from fasting.

The Sixth Wednesday of Great Lent

WE'VE DISCUSSED ST. MARY OF Egypt, who was a rather extreme faster, as she headed out into the desert without food and worked through her repentance all alone. There have been many saints who were called to be hermits like that, to live alone in the desert or the wilderness without comforts. Like St. Mary of Egypt and St. John the Forerunner, they have found that when they live close to nature, without the noise of a town, they can focus on God and really develop their hearts to become very close to him. Today, we'll look at another interesting kind of extreme ascetic hermit, a stylite. Stylites do something very interesting—but we'll get to that in a moment. Let's start at the beginning, with the first stylite ever.

Simeon was born in Cappadocia to Christian parents, and by the time he was thirteen he was a shepherd, tending his father's sheep. He was really very attentive and loving with the sheep and took his job very seriously.

He loved to be in church and to think about God and the teachings of Jesus Christ. He would ask the elders at his monastery lots of questions, and when he was eighteen, he became a monk and devoted himself to strict fasting and unceasing prayer.

He prayed a lot, and he fasted a lot—much more than normal monks. He was so intense that the abbot of the monastery was concerned and told him he needed to settle down a little, to fast and pray a little less, or leave the monastery. People in the monastery live together on the same schedule, but Simeon wasn't part of their schedule—he had his own, much harder schedule to live by. Simeon would not draw back from his efforts, so he left the monastery, found an empty well in the mountains, and lived there where no one would interrupt him, praying and fasting intensely. After a while, the abbot had a dream in which angels told him to bring Simeon back to the monastery, so he did.

Simeon went back to the monastery, but he honestly preferred his time living out in the well as a hermit, so soon he left the monastery again, this time settling in a cave all alone. Truly, he was called to be a hermit and did not wish to live in the monastic community. He preferred to go it alone, trusting only in God.

One year he decided to go the entire forty days of Great Lent without any food or drink, and God preserved him through it, so he started doing that every Great Lent. For the first twenty days he prayed standing up, and then for the second twenty days he would pray sitting down, never eating or drinking a thing.

Simeon's great efforts helped him become very close to God, and people started to know about him. Whole crowds would gather to ask him for healings and to hear some kind of teaching from him. Simeon, like most really holy monks, was trying to remain humble and did not want any worldly glory or fame to distract him from his prayers and his fasting, so he needed to get away from the crowds. He came up with an idea no one had tried before.

He climbed up a pillar about six to eight feet high and settled in. He began to live up on that pillar (where no one could reach him) and to pray and to fast there without interruption. It was a really nice little home for him, and he liked it. After a while, he moved to a taller pillar and liked that better. Then he moved to a taller pillar, and that was even better.

The idea of a monk who lived on a high pillar began to spread, and the Patriarch of Antioch came to visit him. He climbed up the pillar too, and they served the Divine Liturgy up there.

The holy elders living out in the desert heard about St. Simeon and his strange new way of living. They decided to test him. They sent messengers to him, who in the name of the desert Fathers were told to tell St. Simeon to climb down from his pillar. If he refused, that would mean he was disobedient, and they'd forcibly drag him down. But if he agreed and started to climb down, that would mean he was obedient, and they would let him stay up there. Why would it matter if he was obedient? Why would they test him like this? Well, if he was really holy and God was really working in his heart through all of this fasting and sitting on pillars, then that would mean that he would become more loving, more kind, more humble, and more obedient. But if this wasn't real fasting, or if God wasn't the one at work here and something fake or bad was going on, he would become more prideful, and then he would be disobedient. So they were really checking to make sure that God was really working in him and that he wasn't wasting his time and effort.

So the messengers came and demanded that Simeon climb down, and what do you suppose he did? He climbed down—so the messengers stopped him and told him to stay up there.

Over the years, he found bigger pillars until St. Simeon's final pillar was eighty feet tall. He endured many temptations, but prayed to God for help in his struggles. Many people were inspired by his prayerfulness and zeal and by the fact that God took care of him up there. A young monk named Daniel came and visited him and was inspired to find a pillar of his own. He asked St. Simeon for a blessing, and then there were two stylites. Daniel stood on various pillars for thirty-three years of his life, never moving regardless of the weather. Once, his friends came out to find him covered in ice, having stood on his pillar through a terrible storm. The emperor would bring his royal guests to meet the holy Daniel, and he asked Daniel's advice many times.

Saint Simeon spoke wonderful words of Christian wisdom, so the people would wait at the bottom of the pillar for him to come and speak to them. He had gained great wisdom from the Holy Spirit through his prayers and fasting. When St. Simeon was eighty years old and was still up there on the pillar, there came a time when he did not come out to speak to the people for three days. That was unusual. His friend Anthony was worried about him, so he climbed up to check on him. After forty-seven years of living on pillars, St. Simeon had died right there, kneeling in prayer on that pillar.

The Patriarch of Antioch led his funeral. Many, many people came, and they buried him in a grave near his pillar.

For many years, especially in the medieval period, certain monks would be called to live on pillars. We started to call them stylites, which comes from the Greek word *stulos*, meaning "pillar."

In modern times, there have not been many stylites. However, in modern-day Georgia (not the state, but the country in Eurasia, near Russia and Armenia and Turkey), there is an Orthodox monk who is a stylite. A very old stone pillar exists there—a natural formation that goes very high up in the air. Many centuries ago someone built a little church on top of it and lived there as a stylite, and some people climbed up there in the 1940s and found his bones and buried them in a chapel in the church. About twenty years ago, a monk named Maxime Qavtaradze decided to move into that church and live as a modern stylite. He restored the church and now lives up on this huge pillar. Someone made a documentary about him, available online at www.thestylite.com.

The site contains photos that show that the pillar he lives on is pretty big—both very tall and wide so that a little church can fit on top.

Most of the ancient stylites lived on much smaller pillars. They were like little towers, and the top would have short walls around it so that they could stay up there without falling. They were really very small spaces so that the ascetic could live as simply as possible. The stylites are a wonderful example of how fasting can be about more than just food—we can fast from comfort and from easy living. Our fast can be about removing all distractions and leaving ourselves to focus only on prayer so that our hearts are filled with only God.

Holy stylites, pray for us!

༃

When Simeon first went to the monastery, the abbot was worried that he was too intense. Why?

He prayed much more than the other monks and fasted much more intensely.

What made Simeon decide to climb up on a pillar and live there?

The crowds of people were coming to him to be healed and to hear some words of wisdom, and he needed to be a little more out of their reach so that he could focus on prayer.

Why were the desert elders interested in testing whether Simeon was obedient or not?

If God was really at work with him in his fasting, then he would grow more humble and obedient, but they were checking just in case God was not involved and he had grown prideful and disobedi-ent. (He passed the test.)

FOR DISCUSSION: Saint Simeon inspired many future monks to become stylites, living on pillars in an extreme effort at fasting. Living on a pillar is not for everyone, but is there a way that their lives can inspire us during Great Lent? Are there ways that we might put aside our comforts and, say, get up off the soft couch more often and stand before our icons in prayer? Could they inspire us to focus better during the Holy Week that is coming so soon?

The Sixth Thursday of Great Lent

HAVE YOU EVER WONDERED WHY we like to fast for forty days specifically? We fast for forty days before the feast of Christ's Nativity, and we fast for forty days during Lent (plus Holy Week, of course). Why forty days?

If you think about it, "forty days and forty nights" comes up a lot in the Bible. When Noah was in the ark, it rained for forty days and forty nights, and Moses spent forty days and forty nights on Mt. Sinai when he received the Ten Commandments. But there is one particular part of the Bible that shows us that forty days is a really good length for a fast.

When Jesus was ready to stop living anonymously and to become a public figure, teaching and preaching and doing miracles, the first thing He did was to go to the wilderness near the Jordan River, where St. John the Baptist was, to be baptized. Just as we begin our spiritual lives with baptism, so did He. Do you know what He did next?

St. Luke tells us,

Then Jesus, being filled with the Holy Spirit, returned from the Jordan and was led by the Spirit into the wilderness, being tempted for forty days by the devil. And in those days He ate nothing, and afterward, when they had ended, He was hungry. (Luke 4:1–2)

Right after He was baptized, the Holy Spirit led Jesus into the wilderness, where He fasted for forty days. Jesus is our great example; we all strive to be more like Christ, so naturally we follow His example and fast for forty days.

Jesus was about to begin His work in the world. He began with baptism, and then He fasted for forty days. He teaches us that fasting is a good way to prepare ourselves for something important, which is why we prepare ourselves for a great feast like Holy Pascha with forty days of fasting.

As we have discussed fasting, we have talked about people like St. Mary of Egypt and St. Simeon the Stylite, and in past weeks we considered St. John Climacus and his *Ladder*. All of these great saints have something in common: as they went out into the wilderness and fasted from food and comfort and companionship, they were all tempted. As they fast or as they work their way toward holiness, they are tempted to sinfulness along the way, and they call on God for help in resisting the temptations. As they defeat the temptations, God is helping them defeat their own weakness and sinfulness and become more and more resistant to sin.

Because people are tempted, Jesus was tempted. Saint John Chrysostom writes in his sermon on Matthew 4:

When He had therefore fasted for forty days and for forty nights, and afterwards was hungry, He gave an opportunity to the devil to draw near so that He might teach us through this encounter how we are to overcome and defeat him. This a wrestler also does. For in order to teach his pupils how to win, he himself engages in contests with others, demonstrating on the actual bodies of others that they may learn how to gain the mastery. This is what took place here. For, desiring to draw the devil into contest, He made His hunger known to him. He met him as he approached and, meeting him with the skill which He alone possessed, He once, twice, and a third time threw His enemy to the ground.

Like a coach teaching his wrestlers, Jesus teaches us how to defeat our opponent by showing us. He heads out into the wilderness and fasts, and soon the devil comes to Him with temptations. Watch how Jesus answers every temptation with a quote from the Scriptures. St. Luke continues,

> *And the devil said to Him, "If You are the Son of God, command this stone to become bread."*
>
> *But Jesus answered him, saying, "It is written, 'Man shall not live by bread alone, but by every word of God.'"*
>
> *Then the devil, taking Him up on a high mountain, showed Him all the kingdoms of the world in a moment of time. And the devil said to Him, "All this authority I will give You, and their glory; for this has been delivered to me, and I give it to whomever I wish. Therefore, if You will worship before me, all will be Yours."*
>
> *And Jesus answered and said to him, "Get behind Me, Satan! For it is written, 'You shall worship the LORD your God, and Him only you shall serve.'"*
>
> *Then he brought Him to Jerusalem, set Him on the pinnacle of the temple, and said to Him, "If You are the Son of God, throw Yourself down from here. For it is written:*
>
> *'He shall give His angels charge over you,*
> *To keep you,'*
> *and,*
> *'In their hands they shall bear you up,*
> *Lest you dash your foot against a stone.'"*
>
> *And Jesus answered and said to him, "It has been said, 'You shall not tempt the LORD your God.'"*
>
> *Now when the devil had ended every temptation, he departed from Him until an opportune time.*
>
> *Then Jesus returned in the power of the Spirit to Galilee, and news of Him went out through all the surrounding region. And He taught in their synagogues, being glorified by all. (Luke 4:3–15)*

The devil tempts Jesus, and, of course, Jesus does not fall apart, but He defeats the temptations and the devil. Jesus fasted and then overcame temptation, and He is our example; we are called to fast and to be strong in the face of temptation as He was.

We see that the first temptation the devil brings forth is about food. Christ's hunger does not control Him, but He controls His flesh. We are meant to follow this example.

The devil also tempts Jesus with great earthly power, and Jesus rejects it, preferring only to worship the Lord and to follow the will of God. This shows us what kind of ruler our Lord is: He is not coming to the world to become rich and powerful; He is not here to push us around. He is here in love, and He is teaching us about riches that are far more wonderful than anything this earth has to offer.

We have noticed that Jesus answers the temptations with quotes from the Holy Scriptures. Did you also notice that in that last temptation, the devil quoted the Scriptures back to Jesus to tempt Him? We learn two things here. First, we are learning that we should know the Bible, that we should be studying the Holy Scriptures so that when temptation comes, the Scriptures can help us stay strong and defeat temptation. But second, we are also learning that it's possible to have a wrong interpretation or understanding of the Bible. The devil can use the Scriptures for bad purposes, so we should always be careful and follow the Church and the Fathers to help keep us on track with understanding the meaning and purpose of the Scriptures.

So Christ is baptized in the Jordan, and then the Holy Spirit leads Him out to the wilderness for His fast before He begins His important public ministry work. This is a message to us. We who are baptized in Christ need not be defeated by temptations, because we are also aided by the Holy Spirit. The wilderness is a battleground, and for us, the world is like that—a place where we are tempted and we struggle, but also a place where God helps us to find peace and victory over sin. Christ shows us that fasting will help us to overcome temptations and that our fasting will prepare us for the big challenges ahead of us, just as it prepared Him for His public ministry.

☙

Why do we fast for forty days before the holy feasts of the Nativity of Christ and Holy Pascha?

We are fasting for forty days just as Jesus did before beginning His public ministry.

The devil tempted Jesus with what two things?

First he tempted Jesus with bread and then with worldly power.

How does Jesus answer each temptation?

Jesus answers with quotes from Holy Scripture.

FOR DISCUSSION: Jesus Christ spent forty days fasting in the desert, and we are just about to finish forty days fasting during Great Lent. What temptations did you face? How did you handle them?

The Sixth Friday of Great Lent

TODAY IS THE LAST DAY of Great Lent! Today marks forty days since Clean Monday. Great Lent is ending, but the fast is not over—in fact, things only get more and more exciting and intense from here. This weekend we will celebrate two very special days (Lazarus Saturday and Palm Sunday), and then we'll enter into Holy Week and Pascha. We are almost there!

This week we began with St. Mary of Egypt, so we are exploring the Lenten theme of fasting. Let's finish Great Lent with the instructions for fasting that Jesus gave us in the Bible. He said,

> *When you fast, do not be like the hypocrites, with a sad countenance. For they disfigure their faces that they may appear to men to be fasting. Assuredly, I say to you, they have their reward. But you, when you fast, anoint your head and wash your face, so that you do not appear to men to be fasting, but to your Father who is in the secret place; and your Father who sees in secret will reward you openly. (Matt. 6:16–18)*

Jesus Himself told us how He wants us to fast. He doesn't want us to walk around with a sad face, trying to show off our fasting to everyone. Hypocrites are people who are doing one thing on the outside but something else on the inside. Jesus says that they are always making a big deal of how hard it is to fast. They are not really looking for the heavenly reward of growing closer to God, as they should be. Instead, they're trying to earn an earthly reward—they just want attention, and they're getting that attention. But we should not fast to get attention. We should be fasting to grow closer to God, so we will try to avoid attention and instead focus on Him. We will fast humbly, in secret. God will see our fasting, and He will reward us with the spiritual rewards we are seeking.

This is great advice just before Holy Week. Sometimes it can be very tempting to want to show off a little during Holy Week. When we know people who don't go to church much, we might want to impress them with how *hard* Orthodoxy is. But let's not complain and moan about Holy Week. Let's do as Christ tells us. We'll put a big smile on our faces, and we'll talk about the great joy of Holy Week instead. We'll talk about how beautiful the services are and how we start to lose ourselves in Holy Week and lose track of time. We'll talk about the joy of Pascha that awaits us just around the corner.

Fasting seasons are a good time to practice being quiet about the good things we do. But we really should be quiet about them all the time, quietly doing good in all of our spiritual life. In Matthew 6, Jesus teaches us about getting rewards on earth versus rewards in heaven. He begins by saying that when we give alms, we should not blare trumpets and announce to everyone that we are doing a good deed—we should do it in secret, so that we will be rewarded in heaven. Then He says that we should not pray loudly in order to gain attention—we should do it in secret so that we will be rewarded in heaven. Then, as we just read, He says we shouldn't be making a big deal about how hard our fasting is, but instead we should have a big smile on our faces and let God see our struggle in secret, so that we will be rewarded in heaven. In every part of our spiritual lives, we should avoid attention so that we can have a reward in heaven.

What is a reward on earth?

Maybe it is money and power. I might pretend to be very holy so that people will trust me and let me be in charge of them. But a reward is not always something big like money or power. Sometimes we want attention, or we want people to like us. Jesus keeps saying that if you are trying to get a reward on earth, then you will have it. If all you want is attention, then you might get attention; if all you want is popularity, then you might gain popularity. But you won't get a reward in heaven.

What is a reward in heaven?

This is a mystery, because we don't completely understand heaven. We do know that God can reward our spiritual struggles with spiritual understanding. Sometimes fervent prayer is answered with a good feeling of being in God's presence, or we can feel the peace of God, which makes our whole heart feel peaceful and joyful. The rewards in heaven may be something like that—a spiritual reward that we may not understand but which will bring us great joy. We have to trust in God, that He will reward us in ways that are far more wonderful than anything we could find on earth.

Jesus tells us,

> Do not lay up for yourselves treasures on earth, where moth and rust destroy and where thieves break in and steal; but lay up for yourselves treasures in heaven, where neither moth nor rust destroys and where thieves do not break in and steal. For where your treasure is, there your heart will be also. (Matt. 6:19–21)

We must not worry about earthly rewards, because they don't last forever—whether we desire money or stuff or attention or popularity, all of these things will fade away. Only a reward in heaven will last forever. What's more, Jesus shows us that our hearts will follow our treasures—so if we have treasure in heaven, our hearts will want only heaven. As Christians, we hope to focus our hearts on God, so this would be a very good strategy.

May we continue to build up rewards in heaven as we move into Holy Week and Pascha!

ॐ

How does Jesus say the hypocrites fast?

He says that they disfigure their faces and try to look miserable so that people will see that they are following a super holy fast.

How does Jesus say we should fast?

We should anoint our heads, wash our faces, and look happy so that no one knows we are fasting.

Why would it be better to have rewards in heaven than rewards on earth?

Earthly rewards, like money and stuff and attention and fame, do not last forever, but heavenly rewards are eternal.

FOR DISCUSSION: Here's an idea for understanding rewards in heaven: Have you ever noticed that someone who knows a lot about music might enjoy a concert more than someone who doesn't? Or if you knew a lot about art, you might enjoy going to a museum more than someone else. Or if you know all about sports, you might enjoy the Olympics more than the person next to you. Maybe people who pray, fast, and give alms, and who really dedicate a lot of effort to growing closer to Christ, will have the softest hearts, and those people will be the ones who enjoy heaven the most. What do you think?

The Saturday of Lazarus

G REAT LENT ENDED YESTERDAY, AND today we celebrate Christ's most amazing miracle before the Resurrection. He knew that the time was quickly coming for His arrest and Crucifixion and that He would soon go to Jerusalem to face it. As the time drew near, Jesus learned that His good friend Lazarus had fallen sick and was dying. (You can find this story in the Bible, in the Gospel of John 11:1–44.)

Jesus said, "This sickness is not unto death, but for the glory of God, that the Son of God may be glorified through it."

Jesus loved the whole family—Lazarus and his two sisters, Mary and Martha. But when He heard that Lazarus was sick, He did not rush to heal him. Instead He stayed two more days where He was, and then, when He knew that Lazarus had died, He began the long walk to Bethany.

Jesus could have hurried sooner to His friend to save him from dying, but He chose not to. Instead, the death of Lazarus would be for the glory of God, so Jesus waited.

By the time Jesus and His disciples arrived in Bethany, Lazarus's body had been in the tomb for four days. Now, that's important, because at the time, people believed that if someone had been in the tomb four days, that person was really dead, and the body was decomposing. There could be no mistaking it—a person dead for four days was really and truly dead.

When Jesus arrived, Lazarus's sister Martha ran out to meet Him, and she said to Jesus, "Lord, if You had been here, my brother would not have died. But even now I know that whatever You ask of God, God will give You." She had great faith in Jesus, and she knew that He could have healed her sick brother.

Jesus told her, "Your brother will rise again."

Martha answered, "I know that he will rise again in the resurrection at the last day." She thought Jesus was talking about how someday, everyone would be resurrected again in the Second Coming.

But Jesus said to her, "I am the resurrection and the life. He who believes in Me, though he may die, he shall live. And whoever lives and believes in Me shall never die. Do you believe this?"

And she answered, "Yes, Lord, I believe that You are the Christ, the Son of God, who is to come into the world."

As Jesus spent time with the two sisters and saw them weeping, and their friends weeping with them, the Bible says that "He groaned in the spirit and was troubled." And as they led Him to Lazarus's tomb, we read the shortest sentence in the Bible:

"Jesus wept."

Even though Jesus knew that death could not really hold Lazarus, and that He was about to do something wonderful, He cried. And even though Jesus knows that every time we bury a Christian person, that person is going to have eternal life in heaven, He still weeps with us. Death is sad, and it's sad to Jesus too. He doesn't want us to die; He wants us to have eternal life. Even though He has defeated death, He still weeps with us in our sadness when we lose someone we love.

Then the people there said, "See how He loved him!" They were right. Jesus did love Lazarus very much, and that love made Him weep. He loves every one of us, and our deaths will also make

Him weep. Jesus understands our sadness and our suffering, and He enters into it with us.

At Lazarus's tomb, they rolled back the stone door, and Jesus lifted up His eyes and said, "Father, I thank You that You have heard Me. And I know that You always hear Me, but because of the people who are standing by I said *this*, that they may believe that You sent Me." Then He cried with a loud voice, "Lazarus, come forth!"

Of course, Lazarus had been dead for four days, and yet when Jesus called to him, Lazarus obeyed. He came out of his tomb, still tied up in his graveclothes and with his face wrapped with a cloth. Jesus said to them, "Loose him, and let him go."

In the Bible, we sometimes see that a person who has just died might be brought back to life, but this was the biggest miracle ever: a person dead for four long days, already decaying in the tomb, had been resurrected from the dead. Now the people knew that Jesus had power over death like they had never seen before.

Did you notice that Jesus asked the people to unwrap Lazarus? Jesus can perform miracles any way He likes, and it seems that He likes to have the people do some of the work. In this case, He called to Lazarus, who had to get up and come out of the tomb, and also the people in the crowd had to unwrap him, helping him claim his new life. Jesus likes us to be involved with His miracles so that we are not just His audience, but part of His work here on earth.

ॐ

When Lazarus was dying, Jesus said his sickness was for the glory of God. Did He go directly to Lazarus's house to save his friend?

No, Jesus waited two days, and then after He knew Lazarus was already dead, He left for his house.

When Jesus saw the people crying, He cried too. Why would Jesus cry?

Jesus cries because He is sad when people die, just as we are.

What did Jesus do that showed people the glory of God?

He showed them that He is stronger than death by raising Lazarus from the dead.

FOR DISCUSSION: Now here is an amazing thing to think about: where exactly was Lazarus when Jesus called to him? Was he in the tomb? Sort of. His body was in the tomb, but his soul was in Hades, where all of the dead people were waiting—Adam and Eve, Noah and his family, Abraham and Sarah, Isaac, Jacob, and Joseph. Everyone who had ever lived and died was there in Hades, including Lazarus. Can you imagine what they must have thought when they heard Jesus call down to Lazarus, and when Lazarus actually got up and left Hades to go back to his body and his family?

Palm Sunday: Our Lord's Entry into Jerusalem

TODAY IS PALM SUNDAY, BUT the official name of the feast is the Entrance of our Lord into Jerusalem. We commemorate Christ's glorious entrance into Jerusalem, the Holy City, and at the same time we enter into Holy Week.

Have you ever seen, perhaps on television or in a movie, a scene where a king returned from war and had a victory parade into the capital city? To honor the king's great victory, all of the people come out into the streets to see him. He rides in with his armies behind him, and everyone shouts words of praise. In the time of Christ, they waved palms and laid them on the road before the king, like a red carpet rolled out for an important arrival. This is how a king would enter a city.

Of course, Jesus Christ is the King of kings, but not everyone knew that or acted like it. But on this day, something had changed.

As you remember, yesterday was Lazarus Saturday, and we saw that our Lord went to Bethany and raised His friend Lazarus up from the dead. This was a glorious miracle, and many people were very excited about it. They had heard of Christ's teachings and of all the miracles He was doing, and now He had raised up a man who had lain in the tomb for four days. Then Jesus went to

Jerusalem, where those people came out to meet the Lord and to give Him a king's welcome into the city. The Gospel of Matthew reads:

> *And a very great multitude spread their clothes on the road; others cut down branches from the trees and spread them on the road.*
>
> *Then the multitudes who went before and those who followed cried out, saying: "Hosanna to the Son of David!*
>
> *'Blessed is He who comes in the name of the LORD!'*
>
> *Hosanna in the highest!"*
>
> *And when He had come into Jerusalem, all the city was moved, saying, "Who is this?"*
>
> *So the multitudes said, "This is Jesus, the prophet from Nazareth of Galilee." (Matt. 21:8–11)*

The people welcomed Him with displays of honor and shouts of praise, and today we receive Christ in this same way, acknowledging Him as our King and Lord.

In the Lord's Prayer, we pray, "Thy Kingdom come." As we have said before, these words are like an invitation—*Bring me into Your Kingdom. Let Your Kingdom come be over me.* Christ has told us that the Kingdom of God is at hand—we can simply reach out for it. Today as we welcome our Lord, let us call out an invitation in our hearts: *Lord, be our King. Rule over our hearts.*

∽

In the days of Jesus, how did a victorious king enter a city?

There would be a great procession—the people would throw down palms on the ground, like a red carpet, and he would enter with his armies as the people shouted and honored him.

What miracle were the people excited about on the day Jesus was entering Jerusalem?

They heard that He had raised Lazarus from the dead.

How did Jesus enter the Holy City of Jerusalem?

Jesus entered like a victorious king, as the crowd threw down palms and shouted and praised Him.

FOR DISCUSSION: Earthly kings rode into the city on beautiful chariots and grand, expensive horses. They were trying to impress everyone with their wealth. When Jesus entered into Jerusalem, he rode on the colt of a donkey—a poor man's animal. Jesus Christ is the King of kings, and yet He is always humble in this way. Can you think of other ways that He is different from what we would expect in a rich earthly King? What does this teach us about what is truly important in this world?

Holy Monday

O N GREAT AND HOLY MONDAY the Church commemo-
rates the cursing of the fig tree. Jesus often teaches with
parables, which are stories that teach a lesson or a truth. Here,
Jesus is not telling a story, but He offers us a kind of living parable, a parable in action.

In the Gospel of St. Matthew, we read that on the morning
after His entrance into Jerusalem, our Lord found a fig tree by
the road:

> Now in the morning, as He returned to the city, He was hungry. And seeing a
> fig tree by the road, He came to it and found nothing on it but leaves, and said
> to it, "Let no fruit grow on you ever again." Immediately the fig tree withered
> away.
>
> And when the disciples saw it, they marveled, saying, "How did the fig tree
> wither away so soon?"
>
> So Jesus answered and said to them, "Assuredly, I say to you, if you have
> faith and do not doubt, you will not only do what was done to the fig tree, but
> also if you say to this mountain, 'Be removed and be cast into the sea,' it will
> be done. And whatever things you ask in prayer, believing, you will receive."
> (Matt. 21:18–22)

Jesus comes across this fig tree, which is leafy and big and looks
like the kind of tree that would bear a lot of delicious fruit, and
He is hungry. But He finds that this tree has no fruit to offer

Him. It looks fruitful, but it's not, so He curses the tree and it withers, which means that it dries up.

The disciples are fascinated that Jesus can wither a fruit tree with His words, but of course we are not surprised, because Jesus Christ is Lord over all of creation.

But why did He curse this tree? And if this is a parable in action, what does it mean? We see how Christ is telling His disciples that with faith, they can move mountains—when they dedicate their lives to teaching the gospel, God will be at work in them, and through Him, they will do miracles.

We are all called to live fruitful Christian lives. Through prayer, fasting, and almsgiving, by loving God and our neighbor with all our hearts, our lives will be completely changed by God's grace. When we are finally judged by our Lord, He will see the fruit of these efforts—our soft hearts and the love we have shown to the people He has put in our paths.

But the fig tree didn't produce fruit. It was healthy and strong, with all the blessings that God rains down on all the fig trees, but without fruit. It looked wonderful—perhaps we can say that this tree wanted the earthly reward of looking good on the roadside, and it got that reward. But it did not work for the heavenly rewards that come with bearing spiritual fruit.

And so it withered away. Christ gives us eternal life when we embrace His Light and let it shine through us. But if, like the fig tree, we turn away from fruitfulness, then we are rejecting the eternal life He offers, and we wither up instead.

Jesus saw a big, leafy fig tree on the road. What did He look for in the tree?

He looked for fruit.

What did He find?

Jesus found that this tree did not have any fruit, even though it was big and leafy.

What happened when Jesus cursed the tree?

The tree withered up immediately.

FOR DISCUSSION: When we think of the kinds of fruits Christians might see in their lives, we might consider the fruits of the Holy Spirit. Saint Paul teaches that when the Holy Spirit lives in us, He bears fruit in our hearts: love, joy, peace, patience, kindness, goodness, faithfulness, gentleness, and self-control (Gal. 5:22–25). What are we doing to allow the Holy Spirit into our hearts so that we can have this kind of fruit?

Holy Tuesday

O N HOLY TUESDAY, AS WE enjoy the final night of the beautiful Bridegroom services, we consider Jesus' parable of the ten virgins as told in St. Matthew's Gospel:

> Then the kingdom of heaven shall be likened to ten virgins who took their lamps and went out to meet the bridegroom. Now five of them were wise, and five were foolish. Those who were foolish took their lamps and took no oil with them, but the wise took oil in their vessels with their lamps. But while the bridegroom was delayed, they all slumbered and slept.
>
> And at midnight a cry was heard: "Behold, the bridegroom is coming; go out to meet him!" Then all those virgins arose and trimmed their lamps. And the foolish said to the wise, "Give us some of your oil, for our lamps are going out." But the wise answered, saying, "No, lest there should not be enough for us and you; but go rather to those who sell, and buy for yourselves." And while they went to buy, the bridegroom came, and those who were ready went in with him to the wedding; and the door was shut.
>
> Afterward the other virgins came also, saying, "Lord, Lord, open to us!" But he answered and said, "Assuredly, I say to you, I do not know you."
>
> Watch therefore, for you know neither the day nor the hour in which the Son of Man is coming. (Matt. 25:1–13)

The wise virgins have filled their lamps with oil, and the foolish virgins have not—so even though they are waiting for the bridegroom, and they have lamps, they cannot go with the bridegroom.

The virgins in the story are us—the people—and we are all waiting for our Lord Jesus Christ, our Bridegroom, to take us to the banquet. What is the banquet? Well, the banquet that we hear about in Christ's parables and in our prayers is always the same banquet: it is the great and joyful and abundant banquet of living in the Kingdom of God. We can get a taste of this banquet in Holy Communion, but someday when Christ comes back in the Second Coming, the Great Banquet will be our communion with God in His Kingdom.

Isn't it strange that the people with oil cannot share their oil with the others? So often in the Scriptures, Jesus is telling us to love our neighbors and to take care of our neighbors—why can't the wise virgins just share some oil with the foolish virgins, taking care of their neighbors and helping them get into the Kingdom?

To understand this, we'll have to ask: what is this oil?

Before we can even answer that question, we need to understand that Jesus Christ is the Light, and that light can live in you— you can shine His light forth to light up the world. Your soul is like a lamp for Christ's light. What is the oil that fills that lamp and makes it shine? The oil represents acts of mercy; the oil is your faith and your love and the soft heart that you have cultivated. Those who live their lives dedicated to the Lord, praying and fasting and loving their neighbors, will have lamps full of this oil, so they will be able to shine forth with Christ's light. This oil is their very faith and the virtues they have built up over time.

The foolish virgins have spent their time on this earth sleeping. They have not spent their time praying, fasting, and showing love to the people around them, so they haven't developed love for God or faith in Him. They haven't shown love and mercy to the people around them. They don't have soft hearts. And when the Bridegroom comes and the Great Banquet begins, they won't be ready, because they haven't been developing their spiritual lives. They simply won't have a spiritual life.

We don't know when the Bridegroom will come—the Second Coming of Christ could happen today, or it may not happen for a long time. We just don't know. But we do know that we have today. Today we can pray, today we can fast, today we can show love to the people around us, softening our hearts and building up that supply of oil. When the time comes, no one can give us soft hearts— we will have to work on our hearts now, by loving God and loving one another.

꜅

What is the difference between the wise virgins and the foolish virgins?

The wise virgins brought oil for their lamps, but the foolish virgins did not.

When the bridegroom came in the middle of the night, who could go with Him?

The wise virgins with oil in their lamps could go to the banquet, but the foolish virgins could not.

What does this oil represent?

The oil is acts of mercy and love, faith in God, and a soft heart. The oil is the fruit of a healthy spiritual life.

FOR DISCUSSION: We are coming ever closer to Pascha and to the end of our fast. When you think about continuing to fill your own lamp with oil, what might you do when Pascha is over to make sure that you are building up that oil all the time?

Holy Wednesday

O N HOLY WEDNESDAY, THE CHURCH invites us to consider two people: Mary, the woman who anointed Jesus,
and Judas, the disciple who betrayed the Lord. One inherited
the kingdom, while the other fell into perdition and lost the
Kingdom.

> Then Mary took a pound of very costly oil of spikenard, anointed the feet of
> Jesus, and wiped His feet with her hair. And the house was filled with the fra-
> grance of the oil.
>
> But one of His disciples, Judas Iscariot, Simon's son, who would betray
> Him, said, "Why was this fragrant oil not sold for three hundred denarii and
> given to the poor?" This he said, not that he cared for the poor, but because he
> was a thief, and had the money box; and he used to take what was put in it.
>
> But Jesus said, "Let her alone; she has kept this for the day of My burial.
> For the poor you have with you always, but Me you do not have always." (John
> 12:3–8)

Mary (not the mother of our Lord, but a different woman) went
to a great expense to honor our Lord by anointing Him with precious oil, and Jesus praises her for preparing Him for burial—for
He knows that He is coming closer to His Crucifixion and death.

But one of His disciples, Judas Iscariot, objects to the expensive anointing, claiming that the money should have been given
to the poor. We know that he didn't really care about the poor,

but he wanted the expensive oil sold and the money placed in the money box so that he could steal it, as he often did. Judas had been indulging his greed for quite a long time—and in the Gospel of Mark, this story is followed immediately by:

> *Then Judas Iscariot, one of the twelve, went to the chief priests to betray Him to them. And when they heard it, they were glad, and promised to give him money. So he sought how he might conveniently betray Him. (Mark 14:10–11)*

Judas is so accustomed to stealing from the Lord and the disciples that he is able to take it one step further—he will sell Christ to the high priests for money.

The woman who anoints Jesus repents of her sins and honors God in the best way she can. In contrast, we see Judas Iscariot, who is falling ever deeper into sin. On the one hand, a generous woman becomes forever memorable as the one who anointed our Lord for burial, and on the other hand, one of the Lord's own disciples betrays Him for money.

When we see these two people and their situations, we can imagine ourselves both ways: we hope to be the worshipful woman offering her best gifts to the Lord, and we also know that some-times we choose other things over Christ, acting more like Judas than like Mary.

Today we ask our Lord to help us repent, and to heal us and forgive us.

ॐ

Why did Jesus say this woman had anointed Him with expen-sive oil?

To honor Him and to prepare Him for burial.

What did Judas Iscariot say about the expensive oil? Was he being sincere?

He said it should have been sold and the money given to the poor, but really he just wanted to steal the money.

Judas has been stealing from the money box. What will be his next sin?

He arranges with the high priests to betray Christ for money.

FOR DISCUSSION: As awful as Judas' betrayal is, is it possible that we also betray Christ? Do we put other desires ahead of Him? Do we sometimes choose having more stuff or wanting other people to like us over following Jesus as we should? Today we have the example of His betrayal to consider, and when we find examples of our own betrayals of Christ, let us repent and become like the woman who runs to Him with oil.

Great and Holy Thursday

ON GREAT AND HOLY THURSDAY, we remember the Last Supper, or the Mystical Supper, which is the last meal Jesus shared with His disciples before He was arrested and crucified. We can find this event in the Gospel of Matthew, chapter 26:

> And as they were eating, Jesus took bread, blessed and broke it, and gave it to the disciples and said, "Take, eat; this is My body."
> Then He took the cup, and gave thanks, and gave it to them, saying, "Drink from it, all of you. For this is My blood of the new covenant, which is shed for many for the remission of sins." (Matt. 26:26–28)

These are familiar words to the Orthodox, because we hear them at every Divine Liturgy. Jesus tells us to eat of the bread, which is truly His Body, and to drink of the wine, which is truly His Blood. Every time we receive Holy Communion, we are doing the same thing that He is doing here: we are receiving Jesus into ourselves, into our bodies and our hearts and our souls, so that He can live inside of us.

Human beings need food and drink to live. Isn't it amazing that God uses food and drink to show us that we need Him to live eternally? He comes to us in the familiar forms of bread and wine. Holy Communion brings Jesus into each one of us, and it transforms us—but it doesn't just change us alone. If you think about it, it is really Holy Communion that transforms the Church from being just another group of people into being the Body of Christ. Because He comes into us as a Church, He makes us the Body of Christ. In fact, Holy Communion is truly the center of our life as the Church.

Jesus shared this final meal—the beginning of Holy Communion—with His disciples, and then He did something very interesting. The Gospel of John says that He

> *rose from supper and laid aside His garments, took a towel and girded Himself. After that, He poured water into a basin and began to wash the disciples' feet, and to wipe them with the towel with which He was girded. Then He came to Simon Peter. And Peter said to Him, "Lord, are You washing my feet?"*
>
> *Jesus answered and said to him, "What I am doing you do not understand now, but you will know after this."*
>
> *Peter said to Him, "You shall never wash my feet!"*
>
> *Jesus answered him, "If I do not wash you, you have no part with Me."*
>
> *Simon Peter said to Him, "Lord, not my feet only, but also my hands and my head!" (John 13:4—9)*

Jesus stood up after dinner, wrapped a towel around His waist, and then came to wash the feet of each disciple. Of course, they lived in the desert and wore sandals, so their feet could get very dirty. But whose job do you suppose it was to wash people's feet? It was a job for a lowly servant. If you came to the home of a rich man, the rich man did not wash your feet. He was too important for that, but his servant might come and wash your feet for you.

So after offering His own Body and Blood for us, Jesus stood up and tied a towel around His waist like a servant and came to wash Peter's feet. Peter would not allow it. He was horrified at the idea of treating the Son of God as if He were some kind of lowly servant. But Jesus insisted, and He said to the disciples:

"Do you know what I have done to you? You call Me Teacher and Lord, and you say well, for so I am. If I then, your Lord and Teacher, have washed your feet, you also ought to wash one another's feet. For I have given you an example, that you should do as I have done to you." (John 13:12–15)

Jesus asks us to remember to serve one another, no matter how rich or important we might be. We should never think that we are too important to help another person, because our example, Jesus, is always humble and always serves people out of love.

On this Holy Thursday, may we all think about how Jesus gives Himself to us. We are not worthy of Him, and yet He comes to live in our hearts. May He live inside of us in Holy Communion, and may we follow His example of humble service and great love.

ॐ

What does Jesus say the bread and wine really are?

They are His Body and His Blood.

We need food and drink to live on earth. What kind of food will give us eternal life?

The Body and Blood of Jesus—Holy Communion.

Why did Peter think it was strange that Jesus wanted to wash his feet?

Washing feet is a lowly servant's job, and Peter thought the Son of God was too important to wash his feet. But Jesus loves all of us so much that He is glad to humble Himself to serve us.

FOR DISCUSSION: Isn't there something humble about both of the things Jesus did that night? Jesus allows Himself to enter into bread and wine so that He can enter into us and feed us. And then He ties a towel around his waist and acts like a servant, washing the feet of His disciples. He loves us so much, and there is no room for pride in love. Real love is always humble. In what humble ways do the members of your family show each other love?

Great and Holy Friday

GREAT AND HOLY FRIDAY IS the saddest and most serious day of the whole year, because today we commemorate the sufferings of Christ. This is a long and dark day as we think about the terrible things that Jesus endured on the day that He was crucified.

Today, we spend some time thinking about how Christ willingly suffered for us. People mocked Him and shouted at Him. He was crowned with painful thorns. They beat Him and nailed Him to the Cross. He did nothing to deserve this, and yet this is what human beings did to Him. He could have walked away at any time. He could have struck the people down and destroyed us in anger. But He did not. In fact, Jesus said, "Father, forgive them, for they do not know what they do" (Luke 23:34).

At the beginning of Great Lent, we talked about how God wants us to become more forgiving. We talked about how we pray, "Forgive us our trespasses as we forgive those who trespass against us" with the understanding that somehow, we have to find a way to forgive people as Christ forgives, so that we can be forgiven ourselves.

This very sad day could be called the Day of the Greatest Sin. The very sin that brought death and destruction into the world reaches a terrible height on Holy Friday: mankind kills its own Creator. God came to us, perfect and loving and humble, and we hung Him on a Cross. On a day like today, we can understand how terrible sin really is.

And yet, our Lord Jesus Christ forgives us, even the worst of us. Even on this terrible day as we are hurting Him and mocking Him and killing Him, even at that very moment in all of His pain and suffering, our Lord forgives us. He understands our weakness, and He loves us, and He calls us to follow Him.

Sometimes following Jesus will mean going with Him somewhere like the Cross. It will mean picking up our own crosses—our difficulties and struggles—and trying to bear them as He did. We have talked before about how we can ask God to help us carry our crosses, and we will find that the struggle to stop complaining and to become more patient and loving even as we carry those crosses makes us more like Christ.

Sometimes, like today, we follow Jesus to the Cross. But tomorrow will also come, and so will Pascha, and we will follow Him to the glorious Resurrection. Eternal life and joy lie beyond the Cross. But today we stand before the Cross, and we wait quietly.

 ⸎

What kinds of suffering did Jesus endure?

Among other things, He was mocked, beaten, and crucified.

Could Jesus have fought back? Could He have stopped this?

Yes, but He willingly chose to endure this for us.

How did Jesus react to the people who did this to Him?

He asked God to forgive them.

FOR DISCUSSION: Great Lent is a time when we try to struggle—we try to be more loving, more forgiving, more prayerful. Here, at the end of that struggle, Holy Week brings us to Christ's struggle, to His suffering on the Cross. God is always with us when we struggle, and today we are with Him. What kinds of thoughts do you have as you look at the Holy Cross today? Is it different at the end of Great Lent than it was at the beginning or in the middle?

Great and Holy Saturday

GREAT AND HOLY SATURDAY IS a day of waiting and, truly, already a day of celebration. Yesterday, Christ was wrapped in linen and placed in a Tomb. Today, we focus on that Tomb. This is no ordinary grave. This is not a place of death and decay—instead, it is life-giving. This Tomb is the place of Christ's great victory over death.

Great Saturday is the day between Jesus' death and His Resurrection. Today is full of watchful expectation; our grief and mourning are transforming into joy.

Something really amazing happens today, and it's usually called the Harrowing of Hades. You can see it in the icons of Christ's Resurrection. To understand the Harrowing of Hades, we need to know what Hades is.

Let's go back to where we began—in the Garden of Eden, where a tricky serpent told Eve that she would not die from eating the fruit but would become like a god, knowing both good and evil. He wasn't exactly lying, and he wasn't telling the truth either—he was a trickster. The serpent, the devil, was pretending to be Eve's friend, but really he was planning a way to hurt her and trick her into causing the fall of all creation. After Adam and Eve disobeyed God and invited sin and death into the world, sickness and death became part of our life as humans. Adam and

Eve would die, their children would die, and for all generations, everyone would eventually die.

But where did all those people go when they died? Well, not to heaven and not to hell. They all went together, whether they were good guys or bad guys, whether they loved God or not, to Hades. And the devil was down there, keeping them locked inside.

Until one day, Jesus died on a Cross and entered Hades. The devil let Him in happily, delighted to see that God had become just a man, a weak and mortal human being. The Son of God, attacked by the forces of sin and evil and death, was delivered right there into the devil's hands. The devil was so happy to win the ultimate victory by locking the Son of God into Hades forever.

But Jesus Christ is not just fully man: He is also fully God. God can never be held by death. The gates of Hades close behind Him, and what does Christ do? He rises and breaks open the gates. Hades cannot hold Him, for God is so much bigger and more powerful than death. God is the source of all life, and death simply cannot hold Him. The gates of Hades broke apart, and all of Hades was destroyed.

When Christ tears down those gates, all of those souls—the good and the bad, including Adam and Eve and Abraham and Joseph and the Three Holy Youths and everyone we know from the Old Testament and all of those souls we never heard about—have all been held in Hades, but now they are all free. No longer will the gates of Hades hold them away from God. They are all free now to head for the light, to go to heaven, and to be with God.

And as Hades is destroyed, the devil remains there in the darkness, empty-handed and defeated, as Christ triumphs over him. As our hymns say, Christ has tricked the trickster, because what the devil thought would be his greatest victory turns out to be his terrible defeat.

Saint John Chrysostom wrote such a famous sermon for Pascha that we all repeat it every year. He talks about Hades, and we cry out, "It was embittered!" We mean that Hades and the devil were embittered, meaning that they were made bitter and miserable, because as St. John Chrysostom declares:

> *It took a body, and met God face to face.*
> *It took earth, and encountered Heaven.*
> *It took that which was seen, and fell upon the unseen.*
> *O Death, where is thy sting? O Hell, where is thy victory?*
> *Christ is risen, and thou art overthrown!*
> *Christ is risen, and the demons are fallen!*
> *Christ is risen, and the angels rejoice!*
> *Christ is risen, and life reigns!*
> *Christ is risen, and not one dead remains in the grave.*
>
> *For Christ, being risen from the dead, is become the firstfruits of those who have fallen asleep. To Him be glory and dominion unto ages of ages. Amen.*

৵

Why is Holy Saturday a day of waiting?

Because it is the day between the sadness of Holy Friday and the joy of Pascha.

How did Jesus get in to Hades?

He entered as a dead human being—all dead humans went to Hades.

What happened to Hades when Jesus entered it?

The gates were torn apart, and Hades was destroyed forever.

FOR DISCUSSION: Sometimes people wonder why Christ had to die to save us, but understanding the Harrowing of Hades helps us understand—Jesus died so that He could enter into death and destroy it. Death cannot contain the great Giver of Life, so He breaks it open from inside. What do you think it was like for the people in Hades? Do you suppose that the prophets told them Christ would be coming? Did they see that Lazarus got called back to life? Did they know that Christ was about to come and deliver them from death?

Great and Holy Pascha

CHRIST IS RISEN!

The Great and Holy Feast of Pascha is often called the Feast of feasts because it is the most significant day in the church year. We celebrate the ultimate victory: Christ's defeat of death.

This feast is so big that it cannot be celebrated for just one day, or even three days: for the next forty days, we will enjoy the glow of glorious Pascha. We will call out to one another and to this whole wonderful world, "Christ is risen! Truly He is risen!"

But why forty days? Because Christ didn't simply resurrect on Pascha and then disappear. Sometimes, when we talk about the Resurrection, we think a lot about the empty Tomb—after all, when Mary Magdalene went to the Tomb, Christ's body was gone. But the Tomb was not quite empty: there were two angels sitting there, and they said to her, "Why do you seek the living among the dead? He is not here, but is risen!" (Luke 24:5–6). Then Christ Himself appears to Mary Magdalene. He is not gone, but He is truly alive and walking the earth, having triumphed over death. For forty days He will walk the earth in His resurrected body, so for forty days we will celebrate His great victory. Christ is risen!

At today's Agape Vespers, Orthodox Christians all over the world will read the day's gospel reading in many different languages, because like the apostles, we must go out to the world and preach the good news of the Resurrection to all of the different cultures in all of their different languages. In the reading, the resurrected Jesus Christ appears to His disciples:

> Then, the same day at evening, being the first day of the week, when the doors were shut where the disciples were assembled, for fear of the Jews, Jesus came and stood in the midst, and said to them, "Peace be with you." When He had said this, He showed them His hands and His side. Then the disciples were glad when they saw the Lord.
>
> So Jesus said to them again, "Peace to you! As the Father has sent Me, I also send you." And when He had said this, He breathed on them, and said to them, "Receive the Holy Spirit. If you forgive the sins of any, they are forgiven them; if you retain the sins of any, they are retained." (John 20:19–23)

Jesus breathes the Holy Spirit into them, just as He breathed the breath of life into Adam and Eve when He created human beings. He is creating something: He is transforming a group of disciples into the one true Church and giving them the authority to forgive sins. So when you go to confession, when the priest says that your sins are forgiven, that's really true—because God's forgiveness is pouring through your priest. God is really and truly forgiving your sins through the Church; sins forgiven by the Church on earth are forgiven in heaven. Christ gives authority to His holy Church, making a promise to all of us.

Whenever our priests pray for the Holy Spirit to come into the holy water or for bread and wine to be transformed into Jesus' body and blood, or for our sins to be forgiven, we know that Jesus has promised us that the Church really does have the authority to do these things. When the Church calls out for the Holy Spirit, He comes. When the Church offers the sacraments, God always makes them real. This is the promise of our Lord—and at Pascha we are seeing the beginning of the true Church.

For forty days after His Resurrection, our Lord was with His disciples, preparing them and teaching them. Let's mark those forty days by being aware of His presence and His holy Resurrection all the time. We will greet one another with "Christ is risen!" and we will sing "Christ is risen!" every time we pray, when we bless our food, and when we walk in the sunshine. Glory be to God, for Christ is risen from the dead!

ॐ

How shall we greet one another now that it's Pascha?

Christ is risen!

Why will we continue to celebrate this feast and to use this greeting for forty days?

Because Christ resurrected and then stayed on the earth for forty days after.

How do we know that our sins are forgiven when we go to confession?

Because Christ gave the Church the authority to forgive sins. Anything the Church forgives on earth is forgiven in heaven.

FOR DISCUSSION: Do you think it will be hard to remember to sing "Christ is risen" at prayers or meals? Can you think of things you might do to help the family remember for the whole forty days?

Christ is risen!

Inspiration for Crafts and Activities for Great Lent, Holy Week, and Pascha

Countdown to Pascha Ideas

1. A Path to Pascha: In keeping with the theme of tending the garden, consider creating a sand garden with rock stepping stones, one for each day of Lent and Holy Week, leading all the way to Pascha.

For this countdown, you will need a large, shallow container (a serving tray from store-bought baked goods works well), sand, a candle/holder, and forty-eight smooth stones in a small container. You may also need permanent markers or paint if you wish to decorate or number the stones.

> » Begin by smoothing the sand in the shallow container. Plant the candle, representing the Light of Christ (Pascha), in the center of the container.
> » Set a container of stones beside the sand garden so it is easily accessible each day.
> » Beginning on Clean Monday, on each day of Great Lent and Holy Week add one stone to the sand, creating a path spiraling toward the candle.
> » The last stone should end up right next to the candle and will be placed there on Holy Saturday.

» On Pascha, instead of placing a stone, light the candle, the Light of Christ.

Additional ideas: You may wish to number the stones to help you keep track of where you are in the process (or to help keep track of them if the garden is visited by little hands). Or you may wish to paint the rocks to make them more colorful or to remind you of the theme for the day. In lieu of a rock on Holy Friday, you may wish to plant a small cross in the sand.

2. BLOOMING WREATH: Create a flower wreath that becomes more beautiful each day, just as our lives become more beautiful as we tend the garden of our hearts.

To make this, you will need a grapevine wreath, a bow (we chose green to represent the growth we will experience during Great Lent), colored paper, scissors, twist ties, and buttons or glue. Begin by affixing the bow to the wreath (tie, twist, or hot-glue it in place).

» To make each flower, begin with a square of colorful paper. The size is up to you (and the size of your wreath). Varying sizes of flowers will look lovely together. Fold the square into quarters, then fold the quarters in half, forming a triangle.

» Tightly pinch the corner of the triangle, which is in the center of the square, and cut away the outer portion of the triangle, shaping it into a curve. Unfold the paper to reveal an eight-pointed flower. With the tip of your scissors, poke two holes near the center of the flower. Tuck one end of a twist tie into one hole and the other end through a button, then through the other hole. (If you prefer to not use a button, tuck both ends into the flower's holes, then glue a contrasting paper circle over the twist tie to cover it.)

» Use the twist tie to attach the flower to the wreath.

It is up to your family whether you make one flower each day or make all forty-nine at the beginning of Lent and just add one to the wreath each day. Either way, by the end of Lent, your wreath will be bursting with blooms, just as your hearts are bursting with the joy of having grown closer to Christ during Lent.

Additional ideas: Instead of using only flowers on your wreath, you may wish to occasionally add a leaf. Perhaps you could add a cocoon on Holy Friday to represent Christ's burial and then a butterfly on Pascha to emphasize the beauty of His Resurrection. If your children love to count, mark each flower with a number to indicate which day of Lent it was added to the wreath.

3. LENTEN GARDEN: Plant seeds that will grow along with your family as you tend the garden of your hearts during this Lenten season.

For this countdown, you will need soil, seeds, forty-nine small containers, and a spray bottle with water.

» Before Great Lent begins, fill forty-nine small contain-ers with soil. You will need one for each day of Lent, Holy Week, and Pascha itself.

» Plant a seed or two in a different container every day of Great Lent and Holy Week, planting the last one on Pascha.

» Every day, use a spray bottle to spray the earth in each con-tainer that already contains a seed, and watch for growth.

» When the weather is warm enough, plant your Lenten gar-den plants outside. Be sure to share your excess along the way.

Additional ideas: You may wish to number the containers or decorate them to remind you of the Lenten theme for that day. Perhaps you already have small planting containers on hand, but if not, you can make your own from cardboard egg cartons or folded newspaper. (Both are biodegradable and can just be planted with the seedlings.)

Week One: Forgiveness

THIS WEEK BEGINS WITH FORGIVENESS Sunday, so naturally the theme for the week is forgiveness. Every day we'll explore a story or idea about forgiveness. We'll look at Adam and Eve's Fall in the garden and our own path back to Paradise, we'll read Jesus' Parable of the Unforgiving Servant, and we'll consider how Joseph of the Old Testament teaches about forgiveness and points us toward Pascha. We'll also think about the life of the holy and famously forgiving St. Dionysius of Zakynthos. Throughout the week, we'll consider forgiveness from various angles and learn more about why it's so important in our spiritual lives.

In addition to the daily readings, you might be interested in leading some family projects. You could do an object lesson that demonstrates forgiveness in a visual or hands-on way, or you could do some family crafts asking for or expressing forgiveness.

CRAFTS & ACTIVITIES FOR THIS WEEK

» Why should we forgive? With younger children, this object lesson can help us to explain. Use an empty shoulder bag and heavy hand weights (or cans of food) to illustrate how unforgiveness bogs us down. Ask for a volunteer to shoulder the bag. At the start, the bag should be empty. Ask the rest of the family for suggestions of times when other people need our forgiveness (perhaps they have hurt our feelings, they've lied about us, they take something from us or break something of ours, etc.). For each idea, add a weight or can to the bag. After a while, the bag will become heavy and uncomfortable to carry. When it is full or too heavy for comfort, revisit each suggestion, and ask the person holding the bag to say "I forgive you" instead of holding on to the weight of unforgiveness. As the person does so, remove an item from the bag. Continue until the bag is empty and the person feels free again. Talk about how forgiveness is not easy, but it gives us freedom, and when we choose to forgive others, God also forgives us.

» Why should we forgive? With older children, talk together about the following quotes from saints. Print these quotes, cut them apart, and hand them out to family members. As each quote is read, invite discussion. Ask "What do you think about this quote? Can you relate to it somehow? What does this quote mean for us as a family? Why is forgiveness so important?"

  » *St. Nikolai Velimirovich:* "Absolutely nothing will help us if we are not lenient toward the weaknesses of men and forgive them. For how can we hope that God will forgive us if we do not forgive others?"

  » *St. Silouan the Athonite:* "Christ prayed for those that crucified Him: 'Father, count not this sin against them; they know not what they do.' Archdeacon Stephen prayed for those who stoned him so that the Lord would not judge this sin against them. And so we, if we wish to retain grace, must pray for our enemies. If you do not find pity on a sinner who will suffer in flames, then you do not carry the grace of the Holy Spirit, but rather an evil spirit; and while you yet live, you must free yourself from his clutches through repentance."

  » *St. Tikhon of Zadonsk:* "Do we refuse to forgive? God, too, will refuse to forgive us. As we treat our neighbours, so also does God treat us. The forgiveness or unforgiveness of your sins, then, and hence also your salvation or destruction, depend on you yourself. For without forgiveness of sins there is no salvation. You can see for yourself how serious it is."

After discussing each quote, ask, "Why do you suppose we begin Great Lent with forgiveness?"

» Work together to create a poster to hang in your home featuring the concept of forgiveness. Write the word *Forgive* or *Forgiveness* in large letters on a piece of posterboard. Decorate the board with a collage of magazine pictures of people who look as if they're happily interacting, or with sketches of people forgiving each other for different reasons. If you'd prefer, you could create an artistic rendition of the word itself, using a zentangle approach (colorful doodles around or inside the letters). Or perhaps your family would rather create word art and use the word *forgive* or *forgiveness* as the basis for an acrostic poem or in the context of another poem. Be creative together to create this piece, then hang it where you can all see it and be reminded to forgive.

» Asking for forgiveness is an important part of our Lenten growth. Set out some writing paper, pens, envelopes, and stamps where everyone can access them. Encourage each family member to think of someone who was not at Forgiveness Vespers from whom they also would like to request forgiveness, and to write or draw a note for that person, seal it in the envelope, and deliver or mail it to them. Together experience the peace that comes from having asked forgiveness from those you have wronged.

» Extending forgiveness (whether or not it has been requested of us) is another important part of our Christian growth. Think together as a family of someone to whom your family needs to extend forgiveness: perhaps a neighbor that is always noisy or grouchy, or a family from church that you don't always get along with as well as you'd like, etc. Whether or not they have asked for forgiveness, choose together to extend it to them. Begin by praying for them. Take a step toward demonstrating your forgiveness by anonymously doing something kind for them. Think of something they may really appreciate, and find a way to do it without them knowing that it was your family who did it. Perhaps send them an anonymous note, bake them cookies and deliver them secretly, etc. Together experience the release and joy that come from extending forgiveness to others.

Week Two: Orthodoxy

THIS WEEK WE WILL BE exploring the theme of Orthodoxy and the various things that make our worship distinct
and different—those things that make us stand up and cry out in
church, "This is the Faith of the Apostles, this is the Faith of the
Fathers, this is the Faith of the Orthodox, this is the Faith which
has established the universe."

First, we'll discuss the events we commemorate on the Sunday
of Orthodoxy—we are celebrating the return of the icons to our
churches, but why did they leave in the first place? We'll consider
icons, especially the very first icon ever. One of the great lessons
to come out of the iconoclastic controversies was the Church's
assertion of the importance of the Incarnation of Christ, and how
that is made manifest in our worship. Our God took on human
flesh, and He uses matter as a vehicle to share His grace with us.
We'll talk about that in ways that we can all understand, and then
look at some of those other Orthodox things that give glory to
the Incarnation—making the sign of the cross, burning incense,
lighting candles, and using holy water.

Throughout this week, in addition to the daily readings, you
might also want to enrich your family's experience with some
activities that bring these lessons to life.

CRAFTS & ACTIVITIES FOR THIS WEEK

» Have a family parade of icons in your home. Each family member can carry his/her favorite icon as you process through the house singing "O Lord, save Your people and bless Your inheritance." Then circle up and each tell why you chose the icon that you are carrying. Talk about icons and give each family member the chance to tell why they are glad that icons are part of our Faith.

» Decorate the windows of your home with homemade "stained glass" icons that help you to get ready for Pascha (for example, icons of the Crucifixion, the burial of Christ, the Resurrection, the myrrh-bearing women, etc.). If you do not want to draw your own, search online for printable copies of line-art icons. When you find the ones you want, print them out, color them with crayons, and then apply vegetable oil with a cotton swab until the whole icon is oiled. (Be sure to do all of the coloring before you apply the oil: once oiled, the paper will not accept more color.) The oil causes the paper to become transparent, like stained glass. Hang your artwork in a window to let the light illumine it.

» From early Christian times, Christians have made the sign of the cross often so that they could make every part of their lives holy. Do we do this? Do we make the sign of the cross over our food? Over our work? Over our play? What would happen in our lives if we did? Here is a story of a saint who wanted his life to be holy, so he made the sign of the cross frequently:

> *About a hundred years ago, St. Silouan was traveling on a train. Another passenger in the same car offered him a cigarette. St. Silouan took the cigarette and thanked the passenger. Then the saint asked the other passenger*

to make the sign of the cross along with him before they smoked. You know, just as we make the sign of the cross before we eat a meal. The other passenger was a little confused. He told St. Silouan that it felt weird—maybe not even right—to make the sign of the cross over a cigarette and then smoke it! St. Silouan responded, "Well, if what we are about to do does not go with the sign of the cross, maybe we should not be doing that thing at all!" (Adapted from the book The Sign of the Cross *by Andreas Andreopoulos, pp. 93–94)*

Talk together about this story, and challenge each other to always remember St. Silouan's reply. Every time we are about to do something, we should think about whether or not this thing we're about to do agrees with the sign of the cross or not. If it would be odd to make the sign of the cross and do the thing, probably we should not do that thing at all.

» If you don't already cense your home, this is a great week to start. If your parish has a bookstore, gather the family there after church so that you can smell the different kinds of incense available. While you are there, ask your family why they think there are so many different aromas of incense. Purchase one and take it home to use during or after your family prayers this week. (If your parish does not have a bookstore or does not sell incense, you can purchase some elsewhere, or online.) On Thursday of this week, set a piece of incense on a lit coal and watch it together as it burns. How does the incense change while burning? Watch the smoke. Where does it go? How does incense affect the air around it? Talk about how, when we pray, God changes our hearts, softening them just as the incense softens as it burns. When we pray, our prayers rise to heaven like the smoke of the incense. When we pray, we help to make the world around us more beautiful and more holy, just as the incense makes the air around it smell more beautiful and holy.

» Decorate your paschal candles so that they are ready to "come, receive the light!" when we arrive at Pascha. Acquire your family's candles. (They can be wax candles or, if your children are very young, you may consider using taper-shaped LED candles instead.) Allow family members to decorate their candles with permanent-marker drawings, by pressing bits of colored beeswax onto the candle, or by gluing small decorations onto the candle. When you finish, store the decorated candles in your Pascha basket so that you can easily find them when you need them.

» Purchase small, empty water bottles and make some beautiful holy water bottles for your home. Use permanent marker or stickers to label each bottle with the words *Holy Water*. Decorate the bottles with stickers, glue, permanent marker, yarn or ribbon, colorful paper, etc. Use the decorated bottles to store holy water that you bring home for use at your prayer table.

Week Three: Prayer

S INCE THIS WEEK OPENS WITH the Sunday of St. Gregory Palamas, who defended hesychasm, the prayer of the heart, and the teaching that God can reveal Himself to human beings through His energies, the theme for this week is prayer. We'll begin with the life of St. Gregory Palamas and his teachings about prayer, and we'll consider various different prayers and saints who are known for their prayers.

This week we will be learning together about how our Lord taught us to pray. We will discuss the difference between hard and soft hearts. We'll consider a few prayers that we can practice. We will study the example of young people who continued to pray even though it got them into trouble; we will hear about persevering in prayer; and last but not least, we'll be challenged to give glory to God in all things.

CRAFTS & ACTIVITIES FOR THIS WEEK

» When St. Gregory Palamas was a young monk, he devoted himself to praying the prayer of the heart, or the Jesus Prayer. Talk together as a family about the Jesus Prayer. When should we pray it? Hang a copy (you can write a simple version or decorate a beautiful version) in your prayer corner so that you can practice praying this prayer together as a family.

» To encourage your children to pray, work with each child to create their own personal prayer book. For younger children, purchase an inexpensive 4x6 photo album. Together with your child, select photos that remind them of whom they would like to remember in their prayers (e.g., your church, your priest and other clergy, your city or neighborhood, individual family members, friends, etc.). Print the pictures and insert them in the photo album prayer book. Each day, they can look through their prayer book and say, "Lord, have mercy on __ ," and pray for the person in each picture. For older children, select prayers that you frequently pray together or that the children particularly like, and use those to fill a pocket-sized notebook. (You can make your own with a cardstock cover and a few blank pages stapled inside.) Your child can handwrite or type and print the prayers for his or her prayer book. Children can also have a page or two where they can list names of individuals whom they wish to remember. It's okay to leave some pages blank for them to fill as they discover other prayers that they wish to pray. Encourage your children to keep their prayer books at your prayer corner or in their own private prayer corners, if they have them in their rooms.

» Together as a family, talk about the use of a prayer rope. Does anyone in your family use one regularly? If so, how does it help them? Practice praying the Jesus Prayer with a thirty-three–knot rope. Then, consider making your own together to wear during the rest of Great Lent to remind you to continue to work on praying this wonderful prayer regularly. If you do not know how to tie the knots, there are many tutorials to be found online. If this is too daunting for you, order an already-made prayer rope to use as you pray. If you have small children who like to craft, you could make a beaded version that they can use for prayers. String thirty-two pony beads and a cross bead onto an elastic string and knot it tightly. They can pray the Jesus Prayer for each bead, including the cross.

» Saint John Chrysostom offered a list of twenty-four short prayers meant to be prayed hourly. If you wish to begin praying these hourly prayers, they are listed here. You might want to write these out or print them and post one copy in your prayer corner, another on the fridge, another near the bathroom mirror, etc., so that they are easily accessible wherever you will be in those hours.

THE HOURLY PRAYERS OF ST. JOHN CHRYSOSTOM

1:00 AM O Lord, of Your heavenly bounties, deprive me not.

2:00 AM O Lord, deliver me from the eternal torments.

3:00 AM O Lord, forgive me if I have sinned in my mind or my thought, whether in word or in deed.

4:00 AM O Lord, free me from all ignorance and forgetfulness, from despondency and stony insensibility.

5:00 AM O Lord, deliver me from every temptation.

6:00 AM O Lord, enlighten my heart, which evil desires have darkened.

7:00 AM O Lord, as a man have I sinned, have mercy on me, as the God full of compassion, seeing the feebleness of my soul.

8:00 AM O Lord, send down Your grace to help me, that I may glorify Your name.

9:00 AM O Lord Jesus Christ, write me down in the book of life and grant unto me a good end.

10:00 AM O Lord my God, even if I had not done anything

good before You, help me, in Your grace, to make a good beginning.

11:00 AM   O Lord, sprinkle into my heart the dew of Your grace.

12:00 PM   O Lord of heaven and earth, remember me, Your sinful servant, full of shame and impurity, in Your kingdom. Amen.

1:00 PM   O Lord, receive me in penitence.

2:00 PM   O Lord, forsake me not.

3:00 PM   O Lord, lead me not into misfortune.

4:00 PM   O Lord, quicken in me a good thought.

5:00 PM   O Lord, give me tears and remembrance of death and contrition.

6:00 PM   O Lord, make me solicitous of confessing my sins.

7:00 PM   O Lord, give me humility, chastity, and obedience.

8:00 PM   O Lord, give me patience, magnanimity, and meekness.

9:00 PM   O Lord, implant in me the root of all good—Your fear in my heart.

10:00 PM   O Lord, vouchsafe that I may love You from all my soul and mind and in everything do Your will.

11:00 PM   O Lord, shelter me from certain men, from demons and passions, and from any other unbecoming thing.

12:00 AM   O Lord, You know that You do as You will; let then Your will be done in me, a sinner, for blessed are You unto the ages. Amen.

» If you do not already have modeling clay on hand, purchase some. Set it up in a place where the family can sculpt with it at will throughout the week. As you use the clay, pay attention to how difficult it is to maneuver when it is cold and hard, compared to how easy it is to shape when it is warm and soft. This experience will greatly enhance Tuesday's meditation when we focus on one of St. Gregory Palamas's teachings about how closeness to God through prayer softens the heart of our soul.

Week Four: The Cross/Humility

THIS WEEK BEGINS WITH THE Sunday of the Holy Cross. We will hear the story of how the holy Cross of Christ was found by St. Helena, as well as what happened and how the people reacted when it was found. We will talk about why the Sunday of the Holy Cross is celebrated right in the middle of Great Lent.

Our Lord modeled humility, self-sacrifice, and love for the world when He suffered on the Cross. Because of His example, in addition to the Cross, we will also talk about humility, self-sacrifice, and love for others this week. We will explore what it means to take up our cross and follow Him. We will hear the story of Naaman the Syrian, the commander who had to humble himself to experience God's healing touch. We will study the lives of two humble, self-sacrificing saints: St. Maria of Paris and St. Xenia of St. Petersburg. And finally, we will learn from two more recent holy men, Elder Dobri and Patriarch Pavle, what humility and self-sacrifice can look like.

CRAFTS & ACTIVITIES FOR THIS WEEK

» Together as a family, have a scavenger hunt that will help you to become more aware of the Cross's presence in your life. Talk about the holy Cross and why it is so important to Christians. Ask your children how we venerate the Cross. Then go on a scavenger hunt for crosses in your home. Walk from room to room, looking for crosses and venerating them. You might find real crosses hung on the wall and crosses hidden in the design of a bookcase or window. Sing the troparion of the Feast of the Elevation of the Cross as you go.

O Lord, save Your people and bless Your inheritance,
Granting to Your people victory over all their enemies
And by the power of Your Cross
Preserving Your Kingdom!

» Remind yourselves to take up your cross and follow Christ by making small crosses to carry with you. Look online for a pattern for a simple beaded cross that can become a necklace charm, a keychain, or a zipper pull. Older children may prefer to make theirs with large seed beads, while younger children may prefer using the larger, easier-to-handle plastic pony beads. After you make a cross, keep it in your pocket, on your backpack, attached to your keys, or on your jacket zipper pull to remind you to follow Christ. (Note: If your children enjoy making these, they could make additional ones to hand out anonymously. Anonymous giving builds humility, our other theme for the week.)

» Create some cross-themed art either to put up in your home as a reminder or to give as Pascha gifts. Need inspiration? Find a series of cross art tutorials in a variety of media on the *Orthodox Christian Sunday Church School Teachers* blog. Check out the blog (https://orthodoxchurchschoolteachers.wordpress.com/), search for *cross*, and select the art style you'd like to try. These tutorials are geared toward Sunday church school teachers, but families can certainly benefit from them as well.

» This week's lessons feature the stories of many saints and holy people whose greatness is actually their humility. Talk together as a family about superheroes: what makes them so great? Then talk about the humility of the saints we're learning about this week. In what ways are they like superheroes? How are they different? Work together to begin a poster or scrapbook of humble heroes. Then add pictures, icons, sketches, etc., of humble people whom you know or are reading/learning about. Keep your collection in a place where you can add to it in the future as you learn about or meet other humble people.

» Talk together about humility and self-sacrifice. How can each of us be humble and self-sacrificing? Brainstorm ideas so that each member of the family knows where to begin. Here are a few possible ways to prime the pump:

◊ Let others go before you in line.

◊ Make sure your friend gets to play with your favorite toy.

◊ Take the smallest cookie, piece of pizza, or candy instead of the biggest.

Week Five: The Ladder/Almsgiving

THIS WEEK WE ARE THINKING about the theme of the *Ladder of Divine Ascent* as taught by St. John Climacus. We will begin by learning about St. John's life and why he is called Climacus, or "of the Ladder." We will talk about what it means to renounce the world (rung number one of the *Ladder of Divine Ascent*) and how we who are not monastics can also leave the world behind as we grow toward God. We will look at rungs 16 and 17, which encourage us not to love money or our possessions. The rest of the week will be focused on almsgiving. We will study stories from the Scriptures, including the story of the widow who gave two mites, the story of the rich man and Lazarus, and Ss. Peter and John's gift to the lame man at the temple. We will learn from St. Nikolai Velimirovich how our almsgiving affects Christ. And last, but not least, we will learn from the life of St. Luke of Crimea, who gave generously to the poor throughout his life.

CRAFTS & ACTIVITIES FOR THIS WEEK

» Use a ladder or stairs to talk together about climbing toward God. Study St. John Climacus's steps on the *Ladder of Divine Ascent*. (These can be found online if you do not already have a book listing the steps.) Select a few steps to work on together as a family, especially during the remainder of Great Lent. Print out the steps you wish to work on, or use a marker to write them on masking tape or painter's tape. (Families with young children may want to re-word the steps in simpler language first.) You could invite your children to draw a picture of what the step is about, then use the pictures for this activity instead of words, or include the illustration with the words. Once you have the steps printed/written/drawn, affix them to the front of a few stairsteps or on the rungs of a ladder (placed where you will see it often) in your home. Let these words/pictures remind you to keep climbing.

» St. John Climacus said, "Do not be surprised that you fall every day; do not give up, but stand your ground courageously . . . assuredly, the angel who guards you will honour your patience." As we climb the ladder toward God, of course we will fall off sometimes. Being an Orthodox Christian is all about falling down, getting up again, then falling down, and getting up again, every day of our lives. Talk about how Olympic champions don't just quit when they fall down. They keep going. We need to do the same and also help each other to get up again. Search online for a beautiful example of this. During the 1992 Olympics, runner Derek Redmond was determined to finish his race despite a mid-race injury. Watch the video together and discuss what you see and how it relates to St. John's quote above. Make a copy of the Olympic flag and post it on your fridge to remind your family to get back up again—and to help each other back up—when you fall off the ladder.

» Step 16 of the ladder is "on love of money, or avarice." Work on climbing this step during Great Lent by looking for opportunities to help those less fortunate in your neighborhood. There are many ways to do this. Here's one: Put together a few blessing bags (basic necessities packed in a plastic bag and readily available to give away when you encounter a needy person). If you can't think of what to include, search online for ideas—there are many. After you've packaged the blessing bags, keep them in your car or near the front door of your home, so you can find them quickly to share them with those in need.

» Decorate a family coin box where you can collect alms to give to Food for Hungry People or a similar charity. Start with an empty coffee can. Paint the outside gold and add icons (recycled from an Orthodox catalogue) that are specific to your family (i.e., each family member's patron saint and other saints who are special to your family). Cut a slot in the lid of the can. Place the can where you will see it and remember to add money throughout the rest of Great Lent. Donate your collection at the end of Holy Week.

» Double the good that your family does for others during Great Lent. Encourage your entire family to act selflessly and to notice others who do so. Then, each day, take time to ask the family, "What self-sacrificing thing did you see another member of our family do today?" For each selfless thing that a family member notices someone else doing, they get to add a predetermined amount of money to an alms box (a quarter, a dollar, etc.). Remind each other that selfless acts are most selfless when no one notices, but because we are practicing living in such a way, it is okay for us to notice others doing these good things and then talk about it. At the end of Holy Week, when you add up what you've gathered in the alms box, talk together about how much this money will help people who need it here on earth. Be sure to also talk about how, even though most of the time our selfless acts are unnoticed on earth, the good that we do gathers treasure in heaven, because God is always watching.

Week Six: Fasting/St. Mary of Egypt

THIS WEEK WE ARE THINKING about the theme of fasting, which is well modeled for us by St. Mary of Egypt. We will begin the week by learning about her life. Then we will discover what true fasting is and hear what St. John Chrysostom has to say about it. We will study the life of St. Simeon the Stylite, who fasted from more than just food. We will learn why we fast for forty days and whom we are emulating when we do so. On the last day of Great Lent, we will learn what Jesus taught us about fasting (so that we can keep getting better at it throughout Holy Week). We will close week six with the story of Lazarus as we celebrate Lazarus Saturday together and look forward to beginning Holy Week.

CRAFTS & ACTIVITIES FOR THIS WEEK

» Saint Mary of Egypt was repenting her sins during her time in the desert. What does it mean to repent, and how does repentance make a difference? Here's a little object lesson that can help us answer those questions, using only an empty drinking glass and some water. Begin by holding the glass upside down. State that the glass represents us. Our glass is upside down when we are not living a godly life. When we are living life our own way, not God's way, we are not doing what we should, and God is not able to fill us with Himself. Pour some of the water (which represents God and His good gifts to us) over the upside-down glass. How well does the glass hold the water? It will not hold any of the water. Talk about how we miss out when we are not following God: like the upside-down cup, we miss being filled with Him and the good gifts that He has for us. Ask, "How useful is this glass? Is it doing what it was made to do? Can it give a drink of good water to a thirsty person?" No! Then turn the cup right side up, stating that repentance is a complete change of direction in life. When we repent, we turn our lives around and begin to better follow God and live in a way that is pleasing to Him. Ask, "How does a turnaround like that affect us?" Pour the water again. What happens now? Water fills the "repentant" cup. When we live a repentant, obedient life, God is able to fill us with Himself. Ask, "How useful is the glass now? Is it able to serve the purpose for which it was made?" Yes! It is full of water that a thirsty person can drink. When we repent and follow God, He will fill us, and we can be a blessing to those around us who need Him. Saint Mary of Egypt, pray for us that we will repent as we should!

» Saint Mary of Egypt confessed her sins to Christ in the presence of the Elder Zosimas. We also need to confess our sins. Prepare for confession together as a family, and then partake of the Sacrament of Confession. Being forgiven is a great way to approach Holy Week.

» Talk together about St. John Chrysostom's quote about fasting, "Fasting is wonderful because it tramples our sins like a dirty weed, while it cultivates and raises truth like a flower." This quote really helps us think about how to tend the garden of our hearts. Create a piece of art using the quote. Here are a few ideas you could consider: Write the quote with fancy lettering and frame it. Or copy it neatly onto a blank sheet of cardstock and hammer real flowers around it, allowing the petals to release their natural color into the cardstock. (Look online for tutorials if you are not sure how to do this.) Or make small button flowers that match those on your wreath (if you are using the Blooming Wreath countdown) and affix them around the quote, then hang the quote near your wreath.

» James 1:12 says, "Blessed *is* the man who endures temptation; for when he has been approved, he will receive the crown of life which the Lord has promised to those who love Him." Together as a family, begin to prepare yourselves to counter temptation as Christ did: with scriptures. Below are some scripture verses that can help against temptations. Read them together. Choose one to memorize as a family. Write it down and display it in a place where you will all see it and can read and practice it frequently. When everyone knows that verse by heart, move on to the next. Try to memorize as many as possible. As time passes, revisit previously memorized passages occasionally to keep them fresh in your memories. Be prepared to quote them when you feel tempted.

◊ *1 Corinthians 10:13:* "No temptation has overtaken you except such as is common to man; but God *is* faithful, who will not allow you to be tempted beyond what you are able, but with the temptation will also make the way of escape, that you may be able to bear *it*."

◊ *2 Corinthians 10:4–5:* "For the weapons of our warfare *are* not carnal but mighty in God for pulling down strongholds, casting down arguments and every high thing that exalts itself against the knowledge of God, bringing every thought into captivity to the obedience of Christ."

◊ *James 1:13:* "Let no one say when he is tempted, 'I am tempted by God'; for God cannot be tempted by evil, nor does He Himself tempt anyone."

◊ *Hebrews 4:15:* "For we do not have a High Priest who cannot sympathize with our weaknesses, but was in all *points* tempted as *we are, yet* without sin."

◊ *2 Corinthians 5:17:* "Therefore, if anyone *is* in Christ, *he is* a new creation; old things have passed away; behold, all things have become new."

◊ *Matthew 26:41:* "Watch and pray, lest you enter into temptation. The spirit indeed *is* willing, but the flesh *is* weak."

◊ *Galatians 5:16:* "I say then: Walk in the Spirit, and you shall not fulfill the lust of the flesh."

◊ *James 4:10:* "Humble yourselves in the sight of the Lord, and He will lift you up."

◊ *James 4:7–8:* "Therefore submit to God. Resist the devil and he will flee from you. Draw near to God and He will draw near to you. Cleanse *your* hands, *you* sinners; and purify *your* hearts, *you* double-minded."

◊ *Hebrews 13:5–6:* "For He Himself has said, 'I will never leave you nor forsake you.' So we may boldly say: 'The LORD is my helper; I will not fear. What can man do to me?'"

» Help each other think more deeply about the story of Lazarus by acting it out together. John 11:1–44 contains the whole story. After acting it out, talk about how Lazarus's family must have felt when he died. What about when he was alive again? What do you think Lazarus himself felt when he heard Jesus call him back from the dead? And what about Jesus? He knew what was about to happen later in the week. How do you think He felt, being this close to a death and a resurrection? Why do you think this happened at this time in His ministry?

» Practice folding palm crosses so that you can help if your parish makes them for Palm Sunday. Slender, long strips of paper work well as practice palms. If your parish does not make them, perhaps you want to learn how to do it. You can search online to find video tutorials if you do not know or remember how to make them.

Week Seven: Holy Week

THIS WEEK WE ARE THINKING about Holy Week and living it every day of the week. It is the best week of the entire year. We will begin by talking about Christ's triumphal entry into Jerusalem. We will learn a lesson from a fig tree. Then we will turn our attention to the wise and foolish virgins and learn what oil we should have ready in our souls for when the Bridegroom comes. We will look at Mary, who poured expensive oil on Jesus' feet, and Judas, who wanted the money from that oil, and consider whose life to emulate. We will talk about the Last Supper and what amazing gift began then which still blesses us today. We will ponder our Lord's choice to accept suffering and how He responded to those who afflicted Him. We will finish the week with a day of waiting that is also a day of celebration as we learn about the Harrowing of Hades and what that means for all humans.

CRAFTS & ACTIVITIES FOR THIS WEEK

» Talk about the words/phrases that you will hear during the liturgy celebrating the Triumphal Entry and what they mean (especially *triumphal, hosanna,* and "Blessed is He that cometh in the name of the Lord").

» Prepare for the services of Holy Week ahead of time. Look online for printable guides that explain in simple terms what happens at each service. When you find one that you like, print a copy for your family (or for each child old enough to read it). Read the guide aloud on the way to each service. Older children can read it for themselves.

» Eat figs or Fig Newtons as you read aloud the parable of the fig tree.

» Here's a fun object lesson for the Parable of the Ten Virgins: Give a flashlight (some with good batteries, and some with dead/no batteries: Shh! It's a secret!) to each family member and tell them that when you return, you will all go into the dark basement (or another dark room) to find a hidden treat. Go and hide the treat. Turn out the lights in the room where it is hidden. Return to the family and encourage them to go into the room to hunt for the treat. Those without batteries who did not notice ahead of time will miss out on the search as they look for and/or replace their batteries. As you share the treat, talk about the parable, how this activity relates to it, and why we need to prepare our hearts for Christ.

» Compare the kindness of Mary, who anointed Christ's feet with the sweet-smelling ointment, to the greed of Judas, who wanted the money from the ointment instead of wasting it on Christ. Read the entry for Holy Wednesday and talk about it together. Then, as a family, practice showing kindness to each other by giving each other foot massages with lotion or oil.

» Prepare for the Holy Unction service by talking about it together. Why do we have this service? How can it help us to be better Christians? To help young children pay attention during the service, create a coloring page for each child. Ahead of time, draw a candle with a flame floating above it for each of the sets of readings in the Holy Unction service, a total of seven candles and seven floating flames. During the service, have the child draw a wick (to attach a flame to its candle) for each epistle reading, color one candle for each gospel reading, and color one flame for each prayer for healing. By the end of the evening, each candle should be colorful and have its own wick and flame.

» Discuss the Twelve Gospels service before attending and participating in it. Encourage your children to pay close attention to each Gospel reading. Since the readings are from all four Gospels, each tells a different part of the story. Older children can mark the number of the Gospel reading by tying one knot in a narrow ribbon after each reading, finishing the evening with a ribbon bookmark with twelve knots. Or, if you'd rather, make a half-sheet–sized sketchbook for each child by folding three sheets of paper in half and stapling them together into a booklet. This provides one page for every gospel reading so that your child can draw or write something from that reading on the page.

» What does it mean to lament? Talk about that word with your children and why we call Holy Friday night's service the Lamentations Service. Practice singing a verse of each stasis before the service so that you are all familiar with the tune and can sing along at that part of the service. Note: Warn your children that this service contains "spoilers"—we are so excited about Christ's Resurrection that we begin to talk about it even while lamenting His death. Count the spoilers in tonight's service, and talk about them on the way home from church.

» In Holy Saturday morning's service, we hear the story of Jonah. Sometime during the day, read the story together as a family. Act it out with a toy person and a grocery-bag big fish. How does Jonah's story compare to that of Jesus? What did Jonah do

in his three days in the big fish? What did Christ do during
His three days in the Tomb?

(Note: Holy Saturday is a great day to nap in preparation for
the Pascha service. If it will help your child to nap, use a sheet
to build a big fish or tomb tent over his/her bed. He or she can
rest in there today.)

Great and Holy Pascha

O N PASCHA, WE CELEBRATE THE Resurrection of our Lord. For the coming forty days, we will sing "Christ is risen!" and hold on to the joy of the Resurrection. Here are some ideas to inspire your family on Pascha and throughout the forty days that follow.

CRAFTS & ACTIVITIES FOR THE PASCHAL SEASON

» Work together as a family to prepare the treats for your Pascha basket. Talk together about what you would like to eat, and prepare those things. If you don't know what to include, a quick search online will help you find suggestions of traditional Pascha basket foods.

» Practice answering the Resurrection greeting in a variety of languages. Perhaps your parish has particular greetings in specific languages that you can practice. If you think of it early enough, you may even want to ask your priest to help you learn all of the responses for the languages spoken in your parish. If you want to learn even more of them, search online for more paschal greetings.

» Keep the paschal season alive in your home by how you greet each other and what you sing. Greet each other with "Christ is risen!" every morning. What a glorious way to begin each day, waking up together with that reminder. Sing the paschal troparion every day as part of your mealtime prayers and at family prayer time.

» Plant an indoor mini-garden to remind you of the empty Cross and empty Tomb. Fill the water saucer of a flower pot with dirt, then plant a variety of succulents and/or short groundcovers. Create a tomb with rocks, including a large one to be the stone. Keep this mini-garden in your prayer corner or on your dining room table throughout the paschal season to remind you that Christ is risen.

» Bake rolls that represent the tomb of Christ. Stuffed with a marshmallow, each roll will come out of the oven *empty*, just like Christ's Tomb, since He has risen from the dead. An online search for *Resurrection rolls* will offer you a choice of recipes.

» Make a set of storytelling eggs by fitting a few simple items into each of a dozen plastic eggs. Each egg should contain one item that helps to tell the story of the last week of Christ's life on earth, all the way through His glorious Resurrection. You can create your own. (Think of things such as a toy wine bottle or grapes and piece of bread for the Last Supper, a rooster for the one that crowed after St. Peter denied Christ, a large thorn for the crown of thorns, a piece of purple cloth for His purple robe, etc. Be sure to leave the last egg empty: He is risen!) Allow your children to play with the eggs and retell the story themselves.

About the Authors

ELISSA BJELETICH hosts three popular Ancient Faith Radio podcasts: *Raising Saints, Everyday Orthodox,* and together with Kristina Wenger, *Tending the Garden of Our Hearts.* She is the co-author of *Blueprints for the Little Church: Creating an Orthodox Home* (Ancient Faith Publishing, 2016) and author of *Welcoming the Christ Child: Family Readings for the Nativity Lent* (Sebastian Press, 2017), and *In God's Hands: A Mother's Journey through Her Infant's Critical Illness* (Ancient Faith Publishing, 2013). She serves as the Sunday school director at Transfiguration Greek Orthodox Church. Elissa lives near Austin, Texas, with her husband, Marko, and their five daughters.

KRISTINA WENGER is a mom of two who enjoys interacting with little people. She is an educator who has taught first grade and Sunday church school, homeschooled, and co-founded an educational organization. She works part time for the Antiochian Orthodox Department of Christian Education, managing several of their media ministries and writing curriculum. She is also a storyteller who voices some of Ancient Faith's audiobooks as well as the *Let Us Attend* and *Tending the Garden* podcasts. Kristina and her husband have two grown children and are members of St. John Chrysostom Church, York, PA.

Also from Ancient Faith Publishing

Blueprints for the Little Church:
Creating an Orthodox Home
Elissa Bjeletich & Caleb Shoemaker
How do we as Orthodox parents keep our children in the Church throughout their lives? It all begins with involving them in the life of the Church from birth onward—in the parish and also at home. *Blueprints for the Little Church* provides practical ideas and encouragement—without judgment—for incorporating the primary practices of Orthodox spirituality into your family life at every stage of its growth and throughout the church year.

Heaven Meets Earth:
Celebrating Pascha and the Twelve Feasts
John Kosmas Skinas
Enhance your family's celebration of the Great Feasts of the Orthodox Church with this beautifully designed book. Written for all ages and illustrated with icons and more, the book brings alive each of the Twelve Great Feasts (plus Pascha, the Feast of feasts) with hymns, traditions, Old and New Testament scriptures, explanations of the festal icon, and quotes from the Fathers. A wonderful companion as we journey through the liturgical calendar year after year, deepening our faith one feast at a time.

Parenting Toward the Kingdom:
Orthodox Christian Principles of Child-Rearing
Philip Mamalakis, PhD
The Orthodox Christian tradition is filled with wisdom and guidance about the biblical path of salvation. Yet this guidance

remains largely inaccessible to parents and often disconnected from the parenting challenges we face in our homes. *Parenting Toward the Kingdom* will help you make the connections between the spiritual life as we understand it in the Orthodox Church and the ongoing challenges of raising children. It takes the best child-development research and connects it with the timeless truths of our Christian faith to offer you real strategies for navigating the challenges of daily life.

Raising Them Right: A Saint's Advice on Raising Children
St. Theophan the Recluse
Saint Theophan, while from a different era and country, has an uncanny ability to communicate with modern Westerners. *Raising Them Right* provides both practical and spiritual insight into a variety of practical areas, such as baptism, the spiritual and psychological development of children through their teens, and preserving grace in a child's life.

In God's Hands:
A Mother's Journey through Her Infant's Critical Illness
Elissa Bjeletich
Elissa tells the story of her youngest daughter's battle with liver disease, showing how her doubt, fear, and impatience gave way to faith in God's providence.

Ancient Faith Publishing hopes you have enjoyed and benefited from this book. The proceeds from the sales of our books only partially cover the costs of operating our nonprofit ministry—which includes both the work of **Ancient Faith Publishing** and the work of **Ancient Faith Radio.** Your financial support makes it possible to continue this ministry both in print and online. Donations are tax-deductible and can be made at **www.ancientfaith.com.**

To view our other publications,
please log onto our website: **store.ancientfaith.com**

ANCIENT FAITH RADIO

Bringing you Orthodox Christian music, readings,
prayers, teaching, and podcasts 24 hours a day since 2004 at
www.ancientfaith.com